SPIRITUAL CHILDHOOD

SPIRITUAL CHILDHOOD

The Spirituality of St. Thérèse of Lisieux

by

Vernon Johnson

IGNATIUS PRESS   SAN FRANCISCO

Nihil obstat: Edward Mahoney, Censor
Imprimatur: F. Morrogh Bernard
Vicar General, Westminster
February 11, 1953

Vernon Johnson's Scripture quotations are from the
Douay-Rheims version of the Holy Bible

Cover design by Riz Boncan Marsella
Cover photograph of St. Thérèse
courtesy of the Office Central de Lisieux

CONTENTS

PREFACE

LOVE AND SUFFERING. These three words, better than any others, sum up the life of St. Thérèse of Lisieux. To the natural man, when stricken, love and suffering seem totally incompatible. The Christian answer is that so far from being incompatible these two are inseparable and that love is, in fact, made perfect in this world through suffering. We see this focused to a point upon the Cross. The Cross reveals the love of God as inseparably woven with suffering. Suffering is seen to be the expression of the Divine Love precisely because to reconcile men to himself through suffering and to make peace through the Blood of the Cross was the whole object of that Love. That is why in a stricken, suffering world the Cross is our one and only hope, and that is why the Cross has brought healing to millions of souls and will continue to do so as long as this world lasts.

This mystery of love working through suffering did not end with the Cross; it is continued in the world today through the individual members of the Church. In the human body each member is united to the head, and insofar as it is thus united, it is sound in itself and ministers to the well-being of other members. So it is with the Church, Christ's Mystical Body; each member is united to him, its Head, and insofar as it surrenders itself to his redeeming work of love through suffering, so far does it share in the work of its own redemption and also in the redemption of all other members.

God has willed that we as members of the Mystical Body should thus fill up what is lacking in the sufferings of Christ. Although he does not need us at all, he has given us the privilege of carrying on his life and being "other Christs". It is part of his plan that his love should flow through us to other people and that our sufferings when united to his should be redemptive. We are not here to criticize his plan, but we can all see that it is an amazingly beautiful one. If only we did not forget it when we were being hurt! When we think of God, and what he is, the idea of being not only allowed but asked to "help" him makes us dizzy with pride and prostrate with humility.

St. Thérèse, seeing all this, realized that nothing in the way of suffering and sacrifice was too small for God to use, and so gave him everything, with the result that his love streamed through her and she has saved countless souls. This is in brief her "Little Way". In the following pages we shall see her putting it into practice.

The chapters contained in this book appeared originally as a series of articles in *Sicut Parvuli*, the quarterly review of the Association of Priests of St. Thérèse of Lisieux. Every effort has been made to eliminate unnecessary repetitions; if these efforts have not been entirely successful, the reader will realize the situation and will, we hope, be indulgent. The Association of Priests of St. Thérèse is an English-speaking branch of the Pieuse Union Sacerdotale erected by the Holy See in the Chapter of the Carmelites at Lisieux on June 20, 1933.

Vernon Johnson

I

THE FATHERHOOD OF GOD

THE PURPOSE of this book is to try to develop the teaching of St. Thérèse of Lisieux in its relation to our holy
faith and to the Sacred Scriptures. The scene which expresses
most completely the essence of her teaching is to be found in
St. Matthew's Gospel. Our Lord has just returned from one
of his long journeyings with his disciples, those journeyings
in which he was continually teaching them the mysteries of
the kingdom of God. On arriving at the house at Capernaum,
Our Lord asked what it was that they had been discussing on
the road, and St. Mark tells us that they were all silent because
on the road they had been disputing as to who should be the
greatest. Our Lord does not condemn them out of hand; he
knows our human nature too well. He does not even point
out their mistake, but directs their attention to the truth. He
calls a little child to him and takes it in his arms, then, looking upon his apostles, he tells them: *Amen I say to you, unless
you be converted and become as little children, you shall not enter into
the kingdom of heaven.*[1]

St. Thérèse was raised up by Almighty God and canonized
by the Church to be for all the faithful the teacher and model
of the Little Way of Spiritual Childhood. The Little Way was

[1] Mt 18:3.

revealed to her through Scripture and under the guidance of the Holy Spirit, the passage which inspired her most immediately and most profoundly being those words of Our Lord to his apostles: *Unless you be converted and become as little children, you shall not enter into the kingdom of heaven.* With that direct simplicity which is the dominant characteristic of her spirituality, St. Thérèse sweeps aside all accidentals and goes at once to the very heart of religion. Our Lord had said that in order to enter the kingdom of heaven she must become a little child. Now, a little child postulates a father, so St. Thérèse sees at once that if she is to become her heavenly Father's little child, then, for her, God must be before all else a Father. Here then is the starting point of the Little Way—the Fatherhood of God. She will treat God in the supernatural order exactly as a little child treats its father in the natural order, and so, provided she surrenders herself to him, she is safe and nothing can hurt her, for *we know that to them that love God all things work together unto good.*[2] The Little Way is founded upon the truth that God is our Father, and it is in the light of this that St. Thérèse sees all the ups and downs of life, every human experience, including the final one which awaits us all, death.

In all this there is nothing new. The Fatherhood of God is one of the oldest doctrines of the Church. But that is just the difficulty; we are so familiar with the doctrine that we take it for granted, and so miss much of its strength and its intimacy. Almighty God has willed in our own time to make this ancient doctrine live afresh and has chosen St. Thérèse as his instrument. How does she fulfil her mission? Simply by taking Our Lord quite literally: Our Lord did not merely say that she must be converted and become a child; he said she must become a

---

[2] Rom 8:28.

little child. Now a child can have to a certain extent an independent life of its own, calling upon its parent only in moments of need. A *little* child cannot do this: it has no life of its own; it is completely dependent on its parent and so lives with perfect serenity and trust within that parent's protection. For St. Thérèse the word "little", which many would like to eliminate from her teaching, is the key to everything. She has made the Fatherhood of God live afresh for thousands of the faithful by calling us back from being children with a more or less independent life of our own, to become, as Our Lord would have us, *little* children, with no independent life at all, but depending absolutely on our heavenly Father. In so calling us to a fresh realization of the Fatherhood of God, she enables us to move through life with a serenity and confidence which is the prerogative of the childlike soul, for she makes known to us one of those secrets which God hides from the wise and prudent and reveals only to little ones. It is in this sense that the present Bishop of Lisieux is never weary of saying that St. Thérèse has shed a new light on one of the oldest and most fundamental of Catholic doctrines: God is our Father.

Just as a little child, looking upon its father, is not concerned as to whether he is rich or poor, plain or handsome, stupid or clever, but sees only one thing—*father*, so to little Thérèse, as she looked at God, the fact that he was the Creator, the Omnipotent, or the Omnipresent, was purely secondary; to her he was, above all, Father. That God was really and truly her Father was to her the all-absorbing truth. This intimate realization of the Fatherhood of God is vividly expressed in a scene during her life in Carmel. One of the Sisters, wishing to speak with her, knocked at the door of her cell and, on entering, found St. Thérèse sewing, with a rapt expression on her face. "What are you thinking of?" asked the

Sister. St. Thérèse replied: "I was meditating on the Our Father. It is so wonderful to be able to call God 'Our Father'." [3] As she said it, tears came into her eyes. To many this scene may appear emotional or even sentimental, whereas it is profound in its simplicity. It is we who are too complex in our sophistication to fathom its depths. It takes the simplicity of a saint to realize the Fatherhood of God so intimately as to be unable to get beyond the first two words of the *Pater Noster*.

The truth is that the Saint in her simplicity is at the very heart of Scripture. Let us consider this. All down the ages, men have sought to probe the mystery of God and of his nature. In their search they came to think of him as Infinite Truth, Infinite Goodness, and Infinite Beauty. This conception, however, only left them dissatisfied, for it kept God far away; it was not personal enough. Leaving the human heart cold, it could not effectively influence the lives of men. We cannot easily love Infinite Truth, Infinite Goodness, or Infinite Beauty. A few of the prophets had some glimmering of this, but it was not until God became Man that the overwhelming truth was revealed, the truth that God is our Father. From first to last it is the one word out of all others which Our Lord chose, to reveal the character of God to men. The Gospels tell us how Our Lord was praying in the presence of his apostles, and when he ceased, his apostles said to him: Teach us to do that—*Lord, teach us to pray.*[4] And what answer did Our Lord make? He did not say: When you pray, say, O Infinite Truth, Infinite Beauty, Infinite Goodness. He said: *When you pray, say Our Father.* In that moment Our Lord brought the unknown God out of eternity into time, out of the unseen into the seen, out of the unknowable into the lovable, right into the very

---

[3] *Autobiography*, trans. by Canon Taylor (Burns and Oates, 1926), p. 213. (Hereinafter referred to as *Autobiography*.)

[4] Lk 11:1. Cf. Mt 6:9.

hearts and homes of men and women, for we all know what
a father should be. In these two words, "Our Father", lie all
the strength and authority of a Father who is a Creator, all
the love and tenderness of a Creator who is a Father. The
Gospels are full of it. Our Lord's first recorded words spoken
to Our Lady concern the Father: *Did you not know that I must
be about my Father's business?*[5] and his last dying words were:
Father, into thy hands I commend my spirit.[6] And in between, he
was constantly teaching the Fatherhood of God. We will consider two occasions. The first is on the mountainside. Wanting to inspire the men and women around him with a practical
confidence in the Fatherhood of God, he relates it directly to
the material necessities which cause us most anxiety—food
and clothing. In order to drive home his lesson, he who is the
Truth, and therefore the perfect Teacher, draws the attention
of the crowd to something very simple, something which they
can all see and understand. He points to the birds as they fly
overhead: *Behold the birds of the air, for they neither sow, nor do
they reap, nor gather into barns, and your heavenly Father feedeth
them.*[7] Then comes the irresistible argument: *Are not you of
much more value than they?* Not satisfied with only one exposition of his point, he—as all good teachers do—repeats the
same lesson in a rather different form: *Consider the lilies of the
field, how they grow: they labour not, neither do they spin. But I say
to you that not even Solomon in all his glory was arrayed as one of
these. And if the grass of the field, which is today and tomorrow is
cast into the oven, God doth so clothe, how much more you? . . . For
your Father knoweth that you have need of all these things.*

On that first occasion Our Lord teaches confidence in the
Father for material necessities; on the second he teaches the

[5] Lk 2:49.
[6] Lk 23:46.
[7] Mt 6:26.

same confidence in the Fatherhood of God, but this time for spiritual graces. Again he takes simple things as an illustration: *Which of you, if he ask his father bread, will he give him a stone? Or a fish, will he for a fish give him a serpent? Or if he shall ask an egg, will he reach him a scorpion?*[8] Then once again comes the argument: *If you then, being evil, know how to give good gifts to your children, how much more will your Father from heaven give the good Spirit to them that ask him?* As for the rest of Our Lord's teaching, we need draw attention only to the parable of the Prodigal Son. In this parable, which has touched the hearts of men and women perhaps more than any other, and which was one of those most loved by St. Thérèse, the tragedy of sin is seen to lie precisely in this rejection of fatherhood with its consequent loss of sonship, while repentance is symbolized as the return of the son to his father's arms.

The doctrine that God is our Father is not something idealistic and unpractical, quite unrelated to the world in which we live. Our Lord not only taught it, but he lived it out in the midst of the ruthless realism of human life with all its tragedy, its injustice, its suffering and death; and in so doing he has made it possible for the Fatherhood of God to be a living reality for every human being. From the very outset, his public life can be summed up as one continual vindication of the loving providence of the Father. He begins his public ministry as his Father's Son, for at his Baptism there comes a voice from heaven: *Thou art my beloved Son; in thee I am well pleased.*[9] It is within this relationship of Father and Son that Our Lord moves throughout his earthly ministry, but scarcely has he begun his public life than the spirit of the world rises against him. Inevitably so, for, in spite of its vaunted desire for the brotherhood of man, the world does not want the Fatherhood

[8] Lk 11:11–12.
[9] Mk 1:11.

of God, upon which alone the brotherhood of man is based. If the Fatherhood of God is made effective, at once it means authority, and authority means obedience, and obedience means sacrifice. This the world will not have, for the spirit of the world is essentially selfish, independent, and disobedient.

During his Passion the powers of evil closed in upon Our Lord to destroy him. He did not meet the onslaught by counter-attack or elaborate self-defense, but simply by complete abandonment to his Father's loving will and providence: *Amen, amen, I say unto you, the Son cannot do anything of himself but what he seeth the Father doing: for what things soever he doth, these the Son also doth in like manner.... I cannot of myself do any thing. As I hear, so I judge. And my judgment is just; because I seek not my own will but the will of him that sent me.*[10] It is with this assertion of his complete dependence, as Man, upon his Father, that, standing in the Temple courts, he confronts the hatred of the Jews as they compass his destruction. He has no other weapon.

As he draws near to his Cross this calm reliance on his Father's loving providence, so far from being obscured, shines out all the more clearly. To Our Lord the Cross meant simply a going to his Father, who, all the while, held Calvary within the hollow of his hand. There is a calm serenity in the words with which St. John opens the story of the Passion: *Jesus knowing that his hour was come, when he would pass out of this world to the Father... knowing that the Father had given him all things into his hands, and that he came from God and goeth to God, he riseth from supper.*[11] The evening before his death, the theme of his discourse to his apostles was the Father's love for him and his love for the Father, and the Cross as the fulfilment of that love. Some time before, he had told them:

[10] Jn 5:19 30.
[11] Jn 13:1-3.

Therefore doth the Father love me: because I lay down my life.[12]
Now he adds: *That the world may know that I love the Father:
and as the Father hath given me commandment, so do I. Arise, let
us go hence.*[13] And he went straight to his Cross.

On that last evening he had returned to the same theme:
*I came forth from the Father, and am come into the world: again I
leave the world, and I go to the Father.*[14] "Going to his Father",
thus Our Lord sums up his death and Passion. Not so St. Peter.
To him as he sees Our Lord taken prisoner at the entrance to
Gethsemane, it spells complete failure; and to avert this he
draws his sword. He is met by the calm reply: *The chalice which
my Father hath given me, shall I not drink it?*[15] To Our Lord the
Cross is the Father's most precious gift to his beloved Son, and
he accepts it willingly. *Thinkest thou that I cannot ask my Father,
and he will give me presently more than twelve legions of angels?*[16]
Amid the uproar and frenzied fever of the Passion the only
one who moves serenely is the "most beloved" Son of God.
As they nail him to the Cross his first word is *Father, forgive
them, for they know not what they do.*[17] On that same Cross his
last words were *Father, into thy hands I commend my spirit.*[18]
Hanging helpless and dependent, he dominates the scene and
freely surrenders himself into his Father's arms. There is agony
there and desolation,[19] but peace at the end. Never was the
most beloved Son more securely in the bosom of the Father
than when, in the very last moments on the Cross, he cried,

---

[12] Jn 10:17.
[13] Jn 14:31.
[14] Jn 16:28.
[15] Jn 18:11.
[16] Mt 26:53.
[17] Lk 23:34.
[18] Lk 23:46.
[19] For the relation between Our Lord's desolation and the Beatific Vision, see
Tanquerey's explanation, given below in n. 45, p. 125.

Into thy hands, O Lord, I commend my spirit. Yet to those who stood around, the Fatherhood of God seemed to have been lost in darkness. To talk of sonship in such circumstances seemed but an illusion. Indeed the passersby threw it in his teeth: *He trusted in God; let him now deliver him if he will have him. For he said: I am the Son of God.*[20]

Three days afterward the grave is opened, and by it, the "beloved Son", whom we last saw hanging helpless and dying, now stands triumphant. *Go to my brethren,* he says to Mary Magdalen, *and say to them: I ascend to my Father and to your Father, to my God and to your God.*[21] The Cross, which seemed to be irreparable disaster, is revealed as the center of the Father's most exquisite plan for the redemption of his children. Our Lord's death on Calvary reopens the possibility of sonship to men, and the grave becomes the gateway to heaven. Suffering, pain, and death, the results of man's sin and the marks of his separation from his Father, become, through the Passion of Jesus Christ, the stepping-stones which lead us back to heaven. Thus are the tables turned on the devil. The very act of obedience by which, in our human nature, Christ vindicated the Fatherhood of God in the face of the worst the powers of evil could accomplish is seen to be the only means by which we can return effectively to our Father's arms.

The genius of St. Thérèse is that, meditating upon the Passion with the simplicity of a little child, she goes straight to the central point and sees nothing but the Father's merciful love for his children as he gathers them into his arms upon the Cross. Her very simplicity takes her to the heart of Holy Scripture.

Because St. Thérèse is at the heart of Scripture, she is also at the heart of theology, for theology tells us that the object

[20] Mt 27:43.
[21] Jn 20:17.

of the Redemption is to enable us to say once again "Our Father", not merely with our lips but with that complete response of a life in which the will is entirely surrendered to the Father's love. But the restoration of his children to the Father's bosom was not to be achieved by a merely external act, however sublime. It was to be worked out within every single soul by a special gift of the Father's love enabling every child to live by his Father's life, and love with his Father's love, and be, in very fact, a partaker of the Divine Nature.

This gift we know in theology under the beautiful name of *the adoption of sons*, an adoption different from every other adoption of this world, for in no earthly adoption does the child share the very life and so possess the actual likeness of the father who adopts him. To recall us, through her Little Way of Spiritual Childhood, to this central doctrine, as our supreme glory and the foundation of our hope, is the mission entrusted to St. Thérèse. She calls us to regard this doctrine not from the more or less independent standpoint of grown-up men and women, but in the dependent spirit of a little child. In order that she might do this, Almighty God in his providence ordained that she should do nothing great, that she should perform no startling miracles while on earth, but that she should grow to sanctity solely through living as a true child of God within her convent walls. To teach us to say "Our Father" with the complete surrender and dependence of little children is St. Thérèse's great vocation.

In this she is at one with St. Paul, who tells us that to enable us to call God "Our Father" is the supreme work of the Holy Trinity in our souls: *Because you are sons, God hath sent the Spirit of his Son into your hearts, crying: Abba, Father.*[22] To St. Paul as to St. Thérèse this cry of "Abba, Father" is not the cry of more

[22] Gal 4:6.

or less independent men and women; it is the cry of children dependent entirely on their Father. *You have not received the spirit of bondage again in fear: but you have received the spirit of adoption of sons, whereby we cry: Abba, (Father).*[23] It is a cry of confidence, born of the very knowledge of our utter helplessness and a consequent surrender to the Holy Spirit working in us. This is precisely the confidence of which St. Thérèse spoke when she said: "My little way is the way of trust and absolute self-surrender."[24] This cry is far less an articulate utterance than a sob wrung from the heart. To express its intensity St. Paul uses the word "groan": *Ourselves also who have the firstfruits of the Spirit, even we ourselves groan within ourselves, waiting for the adoption of the sons of God.*[25] The whole passage breathes complete helplessness. In our dependence we do not know how to pray, so the Holy Spirit comes to our aid. *Likewise, the Spirit also helpeth our infirmity. For we know not what we should pray for as we ought: but the Spirit himself asketh for us with unspeakable groanings.*[26] In the inmost recesses of our being, the Holy Spirit cries in our hearts,[27] and deep within us stirs that cry of childlike confidence, that cry which no mother can resist in her little one, still less the heavenly Father when he hears it rising from the depths of the truly childlike soul. This is the *De profundis* of the Psalmist, the *Lord, save me* of St. Peter sinking in the sea, the "Our Father" of the Little Way.

This, then, was the Father's plan: to re-establish all things in Christ, giving us the power to say with our whole being: "Our Father"—a thing we had been unable to do ever since the Fall; and so to restore to us everything that through the

[23] Rom 8:15.
[24] *Autobiography*, p. 232.
[25] Rom 8:23.
[26] Rom 8:26.
[27] Cf. Gal 4:6.

Fall we had lost, bestowing upon us sanctifying grace, a life of supernatural love, a partaking of the Divine Nature, a place in the family of our Father, in a word the ability to become again the children of God. When we know God as our Father, heaven has begun on earth, for that is what the life of grace is. Listen again to St. Thérèse: "To call God my Father and to know myself his child, that is heaven to me"[28]—accurate theology in the simple language of the Saint.

At the heart of Scripture and at the heart of theology, St. Thérèse is necessarily at the heart of the Mass. The Mass is the continuation of that sacrifice which restored us to our Father's arms, gave the word "Father" an effective meaning; and it is therefore fitting that the Church should place upon the lips of the priest, as the first prayer to be said aloud after the Consecration in the name of all the faithful, the words "Our Father".

Now that the sacrifice is accomplished, now that the way back to heaven has been opened for us, with complete confidence *audemus dicere Pater Noster*. In this prayer the whole company of the faithful is gathered with the priest into the family of God, fulfilling the destiny for which they were originally created, which was lost through the Fall and is now restored to them for ever. To St. Thérèse, Our Lord's sacrifice, and its continuation in the Mass, was, above all, the heavenly Father's merciful love stooping down from heaven to earth and gathering his children once again into his arms. This indeed is the whole purpose of the Mass.

Finally, since St. Thérèse is at the heart of the Mass, she is at the heart of the priesthood too. The word by which the faithful address the priest is "Father". *As the Father hath sent me, I also send you,*[29] said Our Blessed Lord to his apostles, his

[28] "Mon ciel à moi", *Poems*.
[29] Jn 20:21.

first priests. The mission given by the Father to the Son was precisely this, to restore his erring children to their heavenly Father, by the forgiveness of sins through the sacrifice of the Cross, so that the word "Father" might become a reality to them once again. In this was the merciful love of the Father manifested in all its perfection.

The heart of the priestly vocation is the same, to restore the erring children to their Father through the confessional and the Mass. The priest is God's chosen instrument to continue and apply the plan of his Redemption to the souls of men. The priest, in the language of theology, is ordained to have power over the Actual and the Mystical Body of Christ; in the language of St. Thérèse, to represent and apply the merciful love of the Father.

Our part, our response, is to become childlike. Our Lord said: *Unless you be converted and become as little children, you shall not enter into the kingdom of heaven*, and as he spoke those words he took a little child in his arms. To us today the same voice speaks through the Church. As she speaks, she too directs our attention to a child whom she is holding in her arms. That child is the "little Thérèse" of Lisieux, the great St. Thérèse of the Child Jesus.

II

LOVE (1)

S T. THÉRÈSE LEADS US back to the Fatherhood of God and
throws a new light on the oldest of Catholic truths. With
childlike directness she sees that since Almighty God is her
Father and she his little child, their relationship must be a relationship of love.

God is love, and we have been created by his love solely to
love him and be loved by him. As we have seen, we must love
our heavenly Father in the supernatural order in the same way
as a little child loves its earthly father in the natural order.

In the natural order the love of a little child for its father
is simple, unquestioning, spontaneous, and direct. As it looks
at its father it goes straight to the only thing that matters—
love. His love is everything to the little child, and in return
for it the child can give only one thing, its own love; but in
giving that it gives all, for it is the love of his child alone which
satisfies a father's heart.

In the supernatural order, St. Thérèse's love for her heavenly Father possesses these very characteristics. It was unthink-
able to her that she, the little child whom her heavenly Father
had created solely to love him, should not at every moment
of her life be enveloped in his love. Putting aside all his other
attributes, she goes to the one thing that matters, her heavenly Father's love. "To me He has manifested His Infinite

23

Mercy and in this resplendent mirror I contemplate His other attributes. There, each appears radiant with *love*—His Justice perhaps more than the rest."[1] To St. Thérèse that love was everything: "My little way is all love."[2] And to that overwhelming love there could be only one reply: "O my God, I know it, love is repaid by love alone. Therefore I have sought and I have found, how to ease my heart by giving Thee love for love."[3] "I know of only one means of arriving at perfection, love."[4] "He is in such need of love."[5] "Jesus, I would so love Him, love Him as He has never yet been loved."[6] "I have no other desire unless it be to love Jesus to folly."[7] "Jesus, if the desire of Thy love be so enthralling what joy must the eternal possession of it be?"[8]

The word "love" is so often used for something merely emotional or sentimental that we hesitate to use it in connection with our religion. St. Thérèse rescues us from this false reserve and puts the word "love" again upon our lips in its true meaning.

In the midst of us cold and grown-up lovers, with our love hardened by the difficulty of life, dulled by its dreary routine, stilted by convention, and fettered by human respect, God has placed St. Thérèse, to rescue us from all that is false in our concept of love and lead us back to that simple, direct, spontaneous love which, in the depths of our souls, we really long for.

As we enter the crypt of the basilica at Lisieux, we find ourselves beneath the great arch which spans the entrance to the

---

[1] *Autobiography*, p. 147.
[2] Ibid., p. 372.
[3] Ibid., p. 204.
[4] *Spirit of St. Thérèse*, comp. by Carmelites of Lisieux (Burns and Oates), p. 3.
[5] *Autobiography*, p. 198.
[6] Ibid., p. 353.
[7] Ibid., p. 146.
[8] Ibid., p. 206.

from its mother. To its mother's love ... pacity to
love which exists within its own heart. To her it owes its
existence, with all its faculties of loving; and as it looks upon
its mother's love, its own faculties of loving are quickened
into action, its being goes out in love to its mother. In other
words, the little child loves its mother because the mother
first loved the little child.

If we put this into the supernatural order it gives us an
exact picture of our relation to God. Of ourselves we cannot

[9] Mt 22:37–39.
[10] *Autobiography*, p. 337.

perform a single act of supernatural love; for this we depend entirely on our Father. We love God because he first loved us. Leaving aside his other attributes, St. Thérèse concentrates on this, and her gaze is carried by her simplicity beyond the horizon which limits the outlook of those who are no longer childlike; she sees beyond the complexities of earth which confuse and blur our vision. To her the overwhelming fact was that she had been loved by her heavenly Father from all eternity; that from all eternity God had ordained that she should be created just to love him; that his love for her was from everlasting to everlasting.

Along the ceiling of the crypt at Lisieux there is a scroll on which we find these words of Jeremiah: *I have loved thee with an everlasting love: therefore have I drawn thee, taking pity on thee.*[11] Those words were especially dear to St. Thérèse, because of the simplicity with which they express this eternal truth. With the audacity of a child she makes the words of Our Blessed Lord her own: "I dare to borrow Thine own words, Thy prayer on the last night that saw Thee still a traveller on this earth: *Father, Thou hast loved Me before the creation of the world.*"[12] It is this clarity of vision which gives a timeless stability to her Way. Those who follow it know that they are always supported by the everlasting arms.

Meditating on the plan of our Redemption as it unfolds itself in time, again St. Thérèse goes straight to the motive which underlies it all—the love of the Father, which existed from all eternity. The motive is not God's anger on account of sin, nor God's anxiety that his justice be satisfied; the motive is this—"God so loved". *God so loved the world as to give his only begotten Son.*[13] As she looked with the eyes of a child upon the

[11] Jer 31:3.
[12] *Autobiography*, p. 191.
[13] Jn 3:16.

mysteries of our faith—Bethlehem, Calvary, the Resurrection—she saw only her Father's love.

When we approach the Gospels under the guidance of St. Thérèse, this truth stands out afresh. The words of Our Lord, which, through their familiarity, have largely lost their meaning for us, are seen as if for the first time, and in their full significance.

The Father loveth the Son and sheweth him all things which himself doth.[14] *The Father loveth the Son: and he hath given all things into his hand.*[15] *As the Father hath loved me, I also have loved you. Abide in my love ... as I also have kept my Father's commandments and do abide in his love.*[16] *He that hath my commandments and keepeth them, he it is that loveth me. And he that loveth me shall be loved of my Father, and I will love him and will manifest myself to him.*[17]

These words came from the lips of Our Lord on the eve of his Crucifixion. The task of the world's Redemption lies before him, the network woven by sin is enveloping him, the cruel suffering of the Passion is awaiting him, yet in the midst of all this he is talking only of his Father's love, and far from being ashamed to speak of it in the simplest of terms, he lets us see that to make known that love is the one desire of his Sacred Heart.

This longing of Our Blessed Lord to love and to be loved was, to St. Thérèse, the revelation in time, the outpouring on earth, of that love with which she had been loved before the creation of the world. Throughout her whole life, no matter how complex her problems might be, she was never to cease to speak of this love.

But this Divine Love is not something which she is to

[14] Jn 5:20.
[15] Jn 3:35.
[16] Jn 15:9–10.
[17] Jn 14:21.

follow merely by the force of example; it is to exist in her very soul. She goes directly to the supreme words uttered by Our Lord that evening: *If anyone love me, he will keep my word. And my Father will love him: and we will come to him and will make our abode with him.*[18]

Here was the supreme gift of the Father's love—nothing less than the indwelling of the Trinity in her soul, for, where the Father and the Son are, there also is the Holy Spirit. Her soul was the tabernacle of the Trinity, and she was a partaker in the Divine Nature itself. She was to share in the love with which the three Divine Persons love one another mutually and eternally. She was to live by the life of the Godhead and love with the love of the Godhead. Did not Our Lord pray to the Father on that same night: *... that the love wherewith thou hast loved me may be in them, and I in them.*[19] "O Trinity," she cries, "Thou art the prisoner of my love."[20] Writing to her sister, she says: "He comes and, with Him, come the Father and the Holy Ghost to take possession of our souls."[21] The very life of Christ in her soul was the source of all her power to love the Father with a love worthy of him. Meditating on this, she says: "O my Saviour, it is Thou whom I love; it is Thou who drawest me so irresistibly to Thee, Thou who, descending into this land of exile, wast willing to suffer and to die in order to lift up each single soul and plunge it into the very heart of the Trinity, Love's eternal home."[22]

All this we know. The genius of St. Thérèse is that she invests it with the spontaneous freshness of a little child.

She looks upon her Mother, the Church, in the same way.

[18] Jn 14:23. It was these words which inspired one of the most beautiful of her poems: "Vivre d'amour".

[19] Jn 17:26.

[20] "Vivre d'amour", *Poems*.

[21] *Autobiography*, p. 348.

[22] Ibid., p. 207.

To her the Church is, as the Mystical Body of Christ, above all, the shrine of her Father's love. We have seen that, to St. Thérèse, the whole burden of Scripture is the sending of Jesus by the Father that he may dwell in the soul of his children to restore all that had been lost through the Fall. Similarly, to her, the Church exists for one purpose only, to convey to each individual soul the life of Christ and his power to love.

It was this life that the Church bestowed upon her at her Baptism, making her a child of God, a partaker in the Divine Nature, and heir to heaven. Of this new life, when lost by mortal sin, the Sacrament of Penance was the restoration, and the Blessed Sacrament was the food by which this life was ever nourished. To her the Church was, above all, her Mother, nourishing her with supernatural life and love, restoring her to her Father, and opening the way finally to her home in heaven. To her no other glory of the Church can compare with this—that the Church is the shrine of her Father's love for her, that love which has existed from all eternity.

To this vision of the Church's purpose she will respond with one desire: to cooperate to the utmost with the gift which is offered to her. Her response will be love. "I love my Mother, the Church, and I bear in mind that the least act of pure love is of more value to her than all other works together. But does this pure love really exist in my heart? Are not my boundless desires mere dreams, mere folly?" [23] And what is her answer?

As I meditated on the Mystical Body of Holy Church, I could not recognize myself among any of its members described by St. Paul, or was it not rather that I wished to recognize myself in all? Charity gave me the key to my vocation. I understood that, since the Church is a body composed of different members, she could not lack the

[23] Ibid., p. 206.

most necessary and most nobly endowed of all the bodily
organs. I understood, therefore, that the Church has a heart,
and a heart on fire with love. I saw, too, that love alone
imparts life to all the members, so that, should love ever
fail, apostles would no longer preach the Gospel and martyrs would refuse to shed their blood. Finally, I realized that
love includes every vocation, that love is all things, that love
is eternal, reaching down through the ages and stretching
to the uttermost limits of earth. Overcome with joy, I cried
out: "O Jesus, my Love, my vocation is found at last—my
vocation is love." I have found my place in the bosom of
the Church, and this place, O My God, Thou hast Thyself given to me: in the heart of the Church, my Mother,
I will be Love.[24]

But all this she can be, and do, only because she is the child
of the Church. Of herself she can do nothing. She owes everything to her Mother.

I am a child of Holy Church. I do not ask for riches or
glory, not even the glory of heaven: that belongs by right
to my brothers, the Angels and the Saints. My glory will
be but the reflection of the radiance that streams from my
Mother, the Church. I ask for love. One thought is mine
henceforth, dear Jesus, it is to love Thee.[25]

Sublime though this expression of her love for Christ may
be, she does not stray from reality. Never for one instant does
she take her hand from ours, for the source of this love is common to us all, the supernatural life which throbs throughout
the Mystical Body, and the means by which she proves this
love lies ready to hand for every one of us. "How shall I prove
my love, since love must prove itself by deeds? I, the little one,
will strew flowers. That is the only means of proving my

[24] Ibid., p. 203.
[25] Ibid., p. 205.

love." [26] These flowers, however, are made up of petals which cost dear; her expression is not mere poetry. "I will let no little sacrifice escape me, not a look, not a word. I will make use of the smallest actions and do them all for love." [27] Daily sacrifices, every glance, every word, every single action is to be a means of expressing and augmenting her love: that is the true meaning of her "flowers".

When the ordinariness of these means of sanctity weighs heavy upon her, in her frailty she turns to her Mother, the Church, to help her to do what she cannot do alone.

> Of what avail to Thee are my flowers and my songs, dear Jesus?... Of what avail? I know well that this fragrant shower, these petals of little price, these songs of love from a poor frail heart like mine, will nevertheless be pleasing to Thee. They are but trifles, it is true, yet Thou wilt smile on them. The Church Triumphant, stooping towards her child, will gather up these scattered rose-leaves, and, placing them in Thy divine hands that they may acquire an infinite value, will shower them on the Church Suffering to extinguish the flames, and on the Church Militant to make her triumph. [28]

Here we have that mingling of the poetic and the real that is so truly a mark of childhood. And it is precisely for this that Almighty God has given us St. Thérèse—to invest the ordinary things of life, the actions we perform each day, our minor sacrifices, our words, our looks, with a supernatural value which makes them effective throughout the whole Mystical Body, while our hearts beat with the very love of Christ its Head.

So St. Thérèse rescues us from the dullness of life by making all drudgery divine. She touches all our activities and, however drab they may be, turns them to gold.

[26] Ibid.
[27] Ibid.
[28] Ibid.

For her as for us, the supreme source of this love is the Blessed Sacrament. From the world's point of view there is nothing but the appearance of bread, as simple and ordinary as the simplest and most ordinary things in life: yet it is God. Day after day Christ is there to remind us that it is through the simplest and most ordinary things that he comes to us and desires that we should go to him. From the Blessed Sacrament St. Thérèse learned the reality and condescension of Our Lord's love.

> O my Saviour, Thou ascendest into light inaccessible, yet Thou dost remain in this valley of tears under the appearance of a small white Host in order to nourish our souls with Thine own substance. Let me tell Thee that Thy love runs even unto folly. Before such folly what wilt Thou but that my soul should leap up to Thee? [29]

These words show us clearly that St. Thérèse's life of supernatural love was not based on emotion. Its source was the Blessed Sacrament; and the means by which that truth was grasped was faith, not feeling. Here too, we can follow her, for we have at our disposal this same source of supernatural life. "O Bread of exiles, Host sacred and divine, it is not I that live, my life comes all from Thee." [30]

So St. Thérèse has been given to us as a model in touch with the life we have to live, given to us as an example of what we can become if we faithfully correspond to all Christ is offering us through his Mystical Body, the Church. St. Thérèse is a perfect child of God, because she is a perfect child of the Church.

[29] Ibid., p. 208.
[30] "Jésus, rappelle-toi", Poems.

III

LOVE (2)

WE HAVE HITHERTO considered the simplicity and directness of the supernatural charity of the Little Way: we
must now study, in the person of St. Thérèse, its intimacy.

In St. Thérèse the sense of the tenderness of the heavenly
Father's love was so strong, and has been by her so realistically
expressed, that it has often been considered exaggerated. Such
words as "I have won Him with little caresses, that is why I
shall be so well received",[1] which were spoken by St. Thérèse
on her sick-bed and which are typical of her spirituality, might
easily give a wrong impression. In fact, however, this familiarity, one of the most profound graces of the Little Way,
springs from a close communion with God; it is born amidst
suffering and sacrifice, and is yet in a manner within the reach
of all of us.

In the old convent-garden at Lisieux there stands a tree,
planted not so very long ago. Why was it planted in that particular corner?

Some fifty years since, well within the lifetime of many of
us, St. Thérèse was walking in that garden. It was towards the
end of her life. Weakened by consumption, she was leaning
upon the arm of her sister, Mother Agnes, and in their walk

[1] *Autobiography*, p. 232.

they came to this corner. There a little white hen was shel-
tering its chickens under its wings. St. Thérèse stood spell-
bound, and her eyes filled with tears. Turning to her sister,
she said: "I can't stay here any longer, let us go in." Even when
she reached her cell she could restrain her tears only with
difficulty, and it was some time before she could speak. Then
she said to her sister: "I was thinking of Our Lord and the
touching comparison He chose to bring home to us how tender He is. All my life long He has done that for me, He has
completely hidden me under His wings. I wish I could tell
you all that is in my heart." [2]

We should not miss the significance of this scene.

To St. Thérèse it was no empty image, for it represented
to her the essence of the spiritual life.

This incident did not take place in the first glow of fervour, when she was a novice. It happened when she was weakened by relentless fever, worn out by suffering, and had only
a few weeks to live. At the same time she was enveloped in
great spiritual darkness and beset by perpetual temptations
against the faith. Yet, not in spite of all this but precisely
because of all this, she says: "All my life long He has done that
for me, He has completely hidden me under His wings." St.
Thérèse's tears are not the mark of sentimentality, but of love
fashioned in the school of suffering.

In the natural order there is nothing sentimental in the love
of a mother for her child. With all its tenderness, there is nothing so sacrificial, so self-forgetful, as this love, and it is for this
reason that there is no one so secure as the little child in its
mother's arms. Looked at from this point of view, the scene
we have described can no longer be regarded as superficial or
sentimental; it contains a truth too deep.

[2] Ibid., p. 225.

But more, this image of a mother's love is used in the Scriptures; and through it God himself has chosen to reveal his love for us. *You shall be carried at the breasts. . . . As one whom the mother caresseth, so will I comfort you.*[3] It would be difficult to find words more vividly descriptive of the truth that God's love for us is as tender as the love of a mother caressing her child.

Perhaps more appealing still is the passage in Isaiah where Almighty God goes further and tells us explicitly that his love for us *surpasses* the tenderest love of a mother for her child. *Can a woman forget her infant, so as not to have pity on the son of her womb? And if she should forget, yet will not I forget thee.*[4] In the natural order a mother may conceivably forget her child, but never will the heavenly Father forget *his* children. That is the argument. Meditating on these passages of Scripture, St. Thérèse wrote the following words: "I have long believed that the Lord is more tender than a mother. I have sounded the depths of more than one mother's heart and I know that a mother is ever willing to forgive the little involuntary failings of her child."[5]

The twofold character of the love of Almighty God, its strength and its tenderness, is again revealed by God under the image of the protective love of the mother bird for her young—the very image we are considering. We find it often in the Psalms, and again in one of the most moving scenes recorded in the Gospels.

The children of men shall put their trust under the covert of thy wings.[6] *I shall be protected under the covert of thy wings.*[7] *Under his wings thou shalt trust.*[8] At other times it is the source of his

[3] Is 66:12–13.
[4] Is 49:15.
[5] *Autobiography*, p. 138.
[6] Ps 35:8.
[7] Ps 60:5.
[8] Ps 90:4.

supernatural joy: *I will rejoice under the covert of thy wings.*[9] And each night at Compline the Church calls this image to our minds by bidding her children appeal to God's all-enveloping love for every one of them: *Keep me as the apple of thine eye. Protect me under the shadow of thy wings.*[10]

There are two occasions recorded in the Gospels when Our Lord shed tears—once when standing by the grave of Lazarus, again when looking out over Jerusalem. *When he drew near, seeing the city, he wept over it.*[11] When Our Lord wished to express the greatness of the love which was thus breaking his heart, he used this very image: *Jerusalem, Jerusalem, . . . how often would I have gathered together thy children, as the hen doth gather her chickens under her wings, and thou wouldst not?*[12]

We see now that St. Thérèse in the convent-garden at Lisieux, seeing the image that he had used to make known the love which made him weep, could not but shed tears too—tears of gratitude and joy: born not of ecstasies or visions, but of suffering physical and spiritual, through which her heavenly Father had drawn her to himself. In this embrace of her heavenly Father she had found certain things to be realities which we, with our spiritual sense dulled by an unwillingness to suffer, know only in theory.

She knew that through it all she had been *carried at the breasts*: comforted all the way *as one whom the mother caresseth*: that never, even in the darkest moment, had she been abandoned by a love more tender than a mother's. Under his wings she found security and confidence. She had proved that in the darkest trial of her life there had been, from moment to moment, an adjustment between pain and darkness on the one

[9] Ps 62:8.
[10] Ps 16:8.
[11] Lk 19:41.
[12] Mt 23:37.

hand, and the capacity of her soul to bear it on the other. Speaking of this trial she tells us: "And yet I have never experienced more fully the sweetness and mercy of Our Lord. He did not send this heavy cross when it would, I believe, have discouraged me, but chose a time when I was able to bear it." [13]

At this point we may feel that what was possible for St. Thérèse is quite beyond us, that to be drawn into this embrace of the heavenly Father requires a degree of suffering beyond that which is possible to the ordinary person. Let us then see clearly what it was that enabled St. Thérèse to surrender herself so completely to her Father's love. It was that she became so perfectly his little child.

In this there was nothing ecstatic or extraordinary. "There is no ecstasy", she says, "to which I do not prefer hidden suffering." [14] Confident that she was her Father's little child, and that therefore between him and herself was a relationship of love alone, she made a simple, steady surrender of her will to his in the circumstances of her everyday life. Little mortifications of the will, little disappointments, little interruptions of her plans, little sorrows, little annoyances, little sufferings—these were the material of her sanctity; and it is here that she joins hands with us all, for these are the daily lot of everyone.

She has shared with us too the natural tendency to discouragement, to pride, egotism, irritability, and the manifold miseries which we know so well. They are the very things which we all have to overcome in our own lives. Too often, by continual failure to overcome them, we allow them to take the bloom from our spirituality. We lose the delicacy of our spiritual perceptions, and, worse than that, we lose our

[13] *Autobiography*, p. 158.
[14] Ibid., p. 352.

intimacy with God. But it was not so for St. Thérèse. She accepted these things as being sent straight from God to teach her what she was and her utter dependence upon him. "What does it matter if I fall every moment? By that I learn my weakness, and therein I find great profit. My God, You see what I am, if You don't hold me in Your arms." [15]

Thus, by her Little Way of simple humility and by the daily surrender of her will to his guidance she became so completely dependent that the Father was able to draw her onward through trials which she could not have endured alone right into his arms and to teach her there the tenderness of his love. And that tenderness was revealed to her by the way in which he proportioned every trial to the immediate state of her soul.

By a continual surrender to grace in little trials, she learned that just as out of the ruthless cruelty of Calvary there flowed the Precious Blood, so it is through our crosses that we do, in fact, experience the tenderness of the Sacred Heart.

For St. Thérèse, every small sacrifice made in union with Our Blessed Lord increased the love which alone he desires from us. "I have won Him", she says, "with little caresses; that is why I shall be so well received." [16]

[15] Ibid., p. 336.
[16] Ibid., p. 232

IV

THE MERCIFUL LOVE OF GOD[1]

WE, THEREFORE, adopt as our own the prayer of the new St. Thérèse with which she ends her invaluable auto-biography: 'O Jesus, we beseech Thee to cast Thy glance upon a vast number of little souls, and to choose in this world a legion of little victims worthy of Thy love. Amen'."[2] With these words Pope Pius XI concluded his homily at the Canonization of St. Thérèse. The word "victim" may cause misgiving to some, though this should not be so, for Our Lord was a Victim, and it is enough for the disciple to be as his Master. Every one of us is clearly called to be a victim too. Our Lord is quite explicit on this point: *If any man will come after me, let him deny himself, and take up his cross daily, and follow me.*[3] Clearly those words "little victims of love" cannot be used of a few elect souls only, for Pope Pius XI prays that they may be *legion.*

Why does the Holy Father use such words on this particular occasion? It is because one of the ways in which St. Thérèse teaches us to love Our Lord is by recalling the

[1] In this chapter the writer has made great use of *The Little Catechism*, a short commentary on the Act of Oblation of St. Thérèse, compiled by the Carmelites of Lisieux (Burns and Oates).

[2] *Autobiography*, p. 274.

[3] Lk 9:23.

fact that to be a "little victim of love" belongs to our everyday life and is, in some degree, well within the compass of us all.

It was St. Thérèse's intimate experience of the heavenly Father's love in the midst of trial and suffering that gave her the particular sensitiveness to the Merciful Love of God which is such a special characteristic of the Little Way. Here, at once, she goes straight to the primary motive in our Redemption, the Father's all-enveloping love. In so doing she delivers us from being so absorbed in our fear of the justice of God that we lose our sense of his mercy. Calvary, the divine plan for the restoration of humanity, does indeed satisfy the rights of Divine Justice, but its first motive was the Merciful Love of God, of which the Cross is the supreme manifestation: *God so loved the world as to give his only begotten Son.*[4]

The result of St. Thérèse's vivid sense of the Merciful Love of God, stooping down to embrace his children in their misery and weakness, was twofold. First, it aroused within her a deep realization of how intensely he desires his children's love: "It is the love of His creatures that the Creator thirsts for; He thirsts for love."[5] Again: "He is in such need of love."[6] To St. Thérèse God's Merciful Love was a flood tide longing to fill men's souls and overflow them, a fire longing to consume the hearts of his children. *I am come to cast fire on the earth. And what will I, but that it be kindled?*[7]

Secondly, and inseparably from this vivid sense of the Father's desire to be loved, there grew in the soul of St. Thérèse an acute consciousness of what the rejection of that love meant to him. To Céline, her sister, she would say: "No,

[4] Jn 3:16.
[5] *Autobiography*, p. 198.
[6] Ibid., p. 337.
[7] Lk 12:49.

God is not much loved." [8] Again: "On every side the Merciful Love is rejected and unknown." [9] What is this but the cry of St. John: *He came unto his own: and his own received him not.* [10]

This twofold sense of the heavenly Father's longing for the love of his children and the utter tragedy of his children's rejection of that love roused in her an overwhelming desire. She would offer herself without reserve to the workings of this Merciful Love so that she might console her heavenly Father by giving him, to the fullest degree, the love which he so desired from her own soul. At the same time she would offer herself to his love that she might win for him the love of countless of his children. This desire took definite shape in her Act of Oblation: "The offering of myself as a victim to the Merciful Love." [11] Let her tell in her own words how she was led to make this Act:

> In the year 1895, I received the grace to understand better than ever how much Jesus desires to be loved. While thinking one day of those who offer themselves as victims to the Justice of God, and who turn aside the punishment due to sinners, taking it upon themselves, I felt such an offering to be both noble and generous. I was very far, nevertheless, from feeling myself drawn to make it, and from the depths of my heart I cried: "O my Divine Master, shall Thy Justice alone find atoning victims? Has not Thy Merciful Love need of them also? On every side it is unknown and rejected . . . those hearts on which Thou wouldst lavish it turn to creatures, and seek their happiness in the miserable satisfaction of a moment, rather than cast themselves into Thy arms—into the fires of Thy infinite Love.

---

[8] *Spirit of St. Thérèse*, comp. by the Carmelites of Lisieux (Burns and Oates), p. 12.

[9] *Autobiography*, p. 148.

[10] Jn 1:11.

[11] The full text of the Act of Oblation will be found at the end of this chapter.

"O my God, must that Love which is disdained lie hidden in Thy heart? It seems to me that if Thou shouldst find souls offering themselves as a holocaust to Thy Love, Thou wouldst consume them rapidly and wouldst be pleased to set free those flames of infinite tenderness now imprisoned in Thy heart.... O Jesus, permit that I may be that happy victim—consume Thy holocaust with the fire of Divine Love!" [12]

Her twofold purpose stands out clearly in the text of the Act of Oblation:

I desire to love Thee and make Thee loved, and to labour for the glory of Thy Church by saving souls here on earth, and by delivering those suffering in Purgatory.... I wish to labour for Thy Love alone, with the sole aim of pleasing Thee, of consoling Thy Sacred Heart, and of saving souls who will love Thee through eternity. [13]

The primary purpose is to console her Saviour. To St. Thérèse the saving of souls is but a secondary intention; she desires it less for their personal happiness than to secure more love for him.

With the trustful humility of a little child, St. Thérèse offers herself to God as an empty vessel, so that he may let the flood tide of his love flow into her; or, to use another of her illustrations, as a holocaust waiting for the burning flames of his love to consume her as he desires. "I offer myself as a victim of holocaust to Thy Merciful Love, imploring Thee to consume me unceasingly and to let the flood tide of Infinite Love pent up in Thee pour into my soul, so that I may become a martyr to Thy Love, O my God." [14]

<hr>

[12] *Autobiography*, p. 148.

[13] Ibid., p. 447.

[14] Ibid., p. 448.

We now see what St. Thérèse meant when she said she wished to be a victim of love. She meant that by a complete surrender to God's love, all her life should be made one with his in order to share his love.[15] Thus "according to the expression of St. Thérèse the martyrdom of her life is the state of soul produced by the infinite tenderness of God overflowing without measure into a human heart necessarily limited."[16] She desires to love greatly, but, being only a creature, can love but little.

At this point most of us will pause, saying: This is not for me. Yet the Holy Father prays that there may be a *legion* of little victims of God's Merciful Love. How can we who are so weak hope to attain this love?

St. Thérèse tells us.

My very weakness makes me dare to offer myself, O Jesus, as victim to Thy Love. In older days only pure and spotless holocausts would be accepted by the Omnipotent God, nor could His Justice be appeased save by the most perfect sacrifices; but now that the law of fear has given way to the law of love, I have been chosen, though a weak and imperfect creature, as Love's victim. And is not the choice a fitting one? Most surely, for in order that Love may be wholly satisfied, it must stoop even unto nothingness, and transform that nothingness into fire.[17]

The secret of being a victim of love lies in the fact that God's Merciful Love, of its very nature, reaches out to those who are farthest away, to draw them to himself. "The weaker we are and the more wretched, the better material we make for His consuming and transfiguring fire."[18] With these words

[15] Cf. *Little Catechism*, p. 9, no. 8.
[16] Ibid., p. 10, no. 10.
[17] *Autobiography*, p. 204.
[18] Ibid., p. 360.

she gathers us all within the compass of her Act of Oblation. There is none so far away, or so weak, that he cannot respond to the prayer of the Holy Father for a legion of little victims of the Merciful Love.

Writing to her sister, St. Thérèse says: "The simple desire to be a victim suffices." [19] What is necessary then on our part is a sincere and persevering desire supported by an unwavering hope of obtaining from God all the graces necessary to return him love for love. This point is vital. God loves those whose desires are very great; he not only desires unbounded love, he commands it. *Thou shalt love the Lord thy God with thy whole heart and with thy whole soul and with thy whole mind.*[20] In fact he bids us love as he does. After this how dare we set bounds to our desire to do so; how can he fail to give us all we need to fulfil it? "I am certain", says St. Thérèse, "that Thou wilt hearken to my desires. My God, I know the more Thou wishest to bestow, the more Thou dost make us desire." [21]

But desire, to be effective, must find definite expression. The victim of God's love must cooperate with that love by ceaselessly striving for greater humility. "In order to enjoy the treasure of the Merciful Love we must humble ourselves, must acknowledge our nothingness; and here is where many a soul draws back." [22]

This is what we find so difficult in the Little Way—we must be "little". This littleness, so far from being a mark of weakness, is the *abneget semetipsum* of the Gospel, that complete self-emptying which Our Lord demands of us all, as the expression of our love. The more self-love there is in our hearts, the less divine love there can be.

[19] Ibid.
[20] Mk 12:30.
[21] *Autobiography*, p. 447.
[22] Ibid., pp. 373–74.

This self-emptying is achieved, not by extraordinary exterior mortifications, but by the inner mortification of our will in every detail of the day. This is more sanctifying than any search for special suffering. St. Thérèse says: "I do not like one thing more than another; whatever God prefers and chooses for me, that is what I like best. It is what He does that I love."[23] She begins her Act of Oblation, not by offering herself specifically to suffering, but simply with these words: "I desire, O my God, to accomplish Thy Will perfectly."[24]

This is the *abneget semetipsum* of Our Lord made real here and now in the most practical manner. By this mortification of self-will the soul is laid open to the incoming flood of infinite tenderness; it is consumed in the flames of Merciful Love. We mortify ourselves that Christ may live more fully in us, that we may share more fully in his love for the Father.

The result of this self-surrender will be complete confidence in the Father. St. Thérèse describes this as "the self-surrender of the little child who sleeps without fear in his father's arms".[25] This is what she means by becoming a "victim", for nothing so completely immolates self in man as to become sincerely little.

Again she says: "This self-surrender alone really delivers the soul into the arms of Jesus."[26] The peace which comes through self-surrender is the direct fruit of humility; it can come in no other way. Our Lord has told us so: *Learn of me, because I am meek, and humble of heart: and you shall find rest to your souls.*[27]

It was God's love alone that gave her the strength to offer herself as a victim of that love. She knew her inability to

[23] *Little Catechism*, p. 25.
[24] Ibid., p. 1.
[25] *Autobiography*, p. 197.
[26] *Little Catechism*, p. 20.
[27] Mt 11:29.

ascend, by her own efforts, even the first steps of the ladder
of sanctity." [28] So, in her Act of Oblation, she turns to the one
and only Source. "I long to be a Saint, but I know that I am
powerless and I implore Thee, O my God, to be Thyself my
sanctity. All our good deeds are stained in Thy sight; I desire
therefore to be clothed with Thine own Justice and to receive
from Thy Love the eternal possession of Thyself." [29] In other
words, it is correspondence with grace which makes it possible to become a little victim of Divine Love; fidelity to the
life of the Holy Trinity within us; fidelity to that created gift
by which we partake in the Divine Nature and become again
the sons of God, children of our Father in heaven.

It is to the Holy Trinity that she addresses her Act of Oblation. "O my God, O most Blessed Trinity, I desire to love
Thee and to make Thee loved." [30]

The Sacraments, and above all the Eucharist, are the means
by which this divine life is nourished here on earth. "With
confidence," St. Thérèse prays, "I call upon Thee to come and
take possession of my soul. I cannot receive Thee in Holy
Communion as often as I would; but, Lord, art Thou not
almighty? Remain in me as in a tabernacle; never leave Thy
little victim." [31]

To cooperate with such an ideal may seem beyond our
powers, but we are not left to our own resources. The centre
of the Mass is the Blessed Sacrament. The High Priest places
himself as the Victim on the altar in order that, in Communion, he may take possession of our souls and enable every
one of us to live *per ipsum et cum ipso et in ipso*.

Describing her First Communion, St. Thérèse says: "I felt

---

[28] *Little Catechism*, pp. 21–22. Cf. *Autobiography*, p. 293.
[29] *Autobiography*, p. 447.
[30] Ibid., p. 447.
[31] Ibid., p. 448.

that I was loved, and I said: 'O Jesus, I love Thee and I give myself to Thee for ever.'"[32] Here, at the age of ten, she begins her Act of Oblation. Her words seem to echo those of St. Paul: *He loved me and delivered himself for me.*[33] To this St. Paul made his own response: *I am even now ready to be sacrificed.*[34]

The fruit of her Act of Oblation to God was a growing love of her neighbour. She tells us that it was after she had made the offering of herself that she received the grace to understand more fully the precept of charity. "I made it my study, above all else, to love God; and it was in loving Him that I gradually discovered the secret of His new commandment: *Little children, love one another as I have loved you.*"[35] This love was a participation in the Divine Love of her Master. "The more I am united to Jesus, the more also do I love my Sisters."[36]

So completely surrendered was she to her heavenly Father that not only did his love flow unhindered through her in her lifetime to those immediately around her, but it has flowed since her death to a legion of little souls. Through her Act of Oblation she has become redemptive throughout the whole Mystical Body.

The same will happen with everyone who surrenders himself to the working of God's love; he will become an unobstructed channel through which it will flow to other souls, that the Father may be more loved. But the surrender demands sacrifice, as the price and expression of love. *Greater love than this no man hath, that a man lay down his life for his friends.*[37]

[32] Ibid., p. 74.
[33] Gal 2:20.
[34] 2 Tim 4:6.
[35] *Autobiography*, p. 162.
[36] Ibid., p. 163.
[37] Jn 15:13.

If only we can lose ourselves in Our Blessed Lord, we shall be able to love others with that quality of charity which rises above the daily petty annoyances and the clash of temperaments so often accentuated where true zeal for the faith is concerned. God's Merciful Love will always be recognizable in us as a love independent of our personal likes and dislikes. Our Lord himself asks us for such love: *Love your enemies: do good to them that hate you: and pray for them that persecute and calumniate you: that you may be the children of your Father who is in heaven, who maketh his sun to rise upon the good and bad, and raineth upon the just and the unjust.*[38] *He is kind to the unthankful, and to the evil. Be you therefore merciful, as your Father also is merciful.*[39]

St. Thérèse closes her *Autobiography* with the prayer that, so far from being a small and select company, the number of little victims may be legion; and the Holy Father concludes his homily at the Canonization of the Saint with this prayer: "We, therefore, adopt as our own the prayer of the new St. Thérèse with which she ends her invaluable autobiography: 'O Jesus, we beseech Thee to cast Thy glance upon a vast number of little souls, and to choose in this world a legion of little victims worthy of Thy Love.' Amen." The Mass of the Saint ends with a prayer that our life throughout the day may be filled by the same love which inspired St. Thérèse to offer herself as a little victim to the Merciful Love of God: "May the heavenly mystery inflame us with that fire of love wherewith Thy virgin saint, Thérèse, offered herself to Thee as a victim of charity for all mankind. Through Our Lord Jesus Christ."

With our Mother, the Church, thus inspiring, directing, and supporting us, and with the Saint herself at our side pray-

[38] Mt 5:44-45.
[39] Lk 6:35-36.

ing with and for us, we cannot say that this is beyond us—to whom Our Blessed Lord has said: *Be you therefore perfect, as also your heavenly Father is perfect.*[40]

————

OFFERING
of St. Thérèse of the Child Jesus
as Victim of Holocaust
to the Merciful Love of God.

O my God, most Blessed Trinity, I desire to love Thee and to make Thee loved, to labour for the glory of Holy Church by saving souls on earth and by delivering those who suffer in Purgatory. I desire to accomplish Thy will perfectly and to attain to the degree of glory which Thou hast prepared for me in Thy Kingdom: in a word, I long to be a Saint, but I know that I am powerless, and I implore Thee, O my God, to be Thyself my sanctity.

Since Thou hast so loved me as to give me Thine only Son to be my Saviour and my Spouse, the infinite treasures of His merits are mine. To Thee I offer them with joy, beseeching Thee to behold me only through the eyes of Jesus and in His heart burning with love.

Again, I offer Thee all the merits of the Saints in heaven and on earth, their acts of love and those of the holy angels. Lastly I offer Thee, O Blessed Trinity, the love and merits of the holy Virgin, my most dear Mother; and to her I entrust my oblation, begging her to present it to Thee. Her Divine Son, my well-beloved Spouse, during the days of His life on earth, told us: *If you ask the Father anything in My name, He will give it to you.* I am then certain that Thou wilt hearken to my

[40] Mt 5:48.

desires.... My God, I know it, the more Thou willest to give, the more dost Thou make us desire. Immense are the desires that I feel within my heart, and with confidence I call upon Thee to come and take possession of my soul. I cannot receive Thee in Holy Communion as often as I would, but Lord, art Thou not almighty?... Remain in me as in the tabernacle, never leave Thy little victim.

I long to console Thee for the ingratitude of the wicked, and I pray Thee to take from me the power to displease Thee. If through frailty I sometimes fall, may Thy divine glance purify my soul immediately, consuming every imperfection, as fire transforms all things into itself.

I thank Thee, O my God, for all the graces Thou hast showered upon me, in particular for having made me pass through the crucible of suffering. With joy shall I behold Thee on the last day bearing Thy sceptre, the Cross. Since Thou hast deigned to give me for my portion this most precious Cross, I hope I may resemble Thee in heaven and see the sacred stigmata of Thy Passion shine on my glorified body.

After this exile on earth, I hope to enjoy possession of Thee in the eternal Fatherland, but I have no wish to amass merits for heaven, I will work for Thy love alone, my sole aim being to give Thee pleasure, to console Thy Sacred Heart, and to save souls who will love Thee for ever.

At the close of this life I shall appear before Thee with empty hands, for I ask not, Lord, that Thou wouldst count my works.... All our good deeds are stained in Thy sight. I desire therefore to be clothed with Thine own Justice, and to receive from Thy Love the eternal possession of Thyself. I crave no other throne, no other crown but Thee, O my Beloved.

In Thy sight, time is nothing; one day is as a thousand years. Thou canst in an instant prepare me to appear before Thee.

That my life may be one act of perfect love, I offer myself as Victim of Holocaust to Thy Merciful Love, imploring Thee to consume me unceasingly, and to let the flood-tide of infinite tenderness pent up in Thee, flow into my soul, that so I may become a martyr of Thy Love, O my God.

May this martyrdom, after having prepared me to appear before Thee, break life's web at last, and may my soul take its flight, unhindered, to the eternal embrace of Thy Merciful Love.

I desire, O my Beloved, at every heart-beat to renew this oblation an infinite number of times, till the shadows fade away and I can tell Thee my love eternally face to face....

(*Signed*) MARIE-FRANÇOISE-THÉRÈSE DE L'ENFANT-JÉSUS
ET DE LA SAINT FACE.
(rel. carm. ind.)
Feast of the most Holy Trinity, the 9th June,
in the year of grace, 1895.

V

HUMILITY (1)

ONE OF THE WAYS in which the devil tries to lessen the influence of the Saint is to make the littleness of the Little Way, which is in fact its strength, appear mere weakness. It gives rise to the fear of sentimentality and so prevents many from really understanding "the greatest Saint of modern times" (Pius X).

There is, however, another and a deeper reason for our shrinking from the word "little"; it strikes at our self-esteem. We do not know what this littleness may involve; we are afraid and keep the Little Way at arm's length, unconscious that we are afraid and that in so doing we are rejecting the very secret of sanctity.

Yet many of those who, at first, have felt a distaste for the littleness of St. Thérèse have, after a patient pursuit of the Little Way, found it to be the greatest possible support in some acute crisis of their lives.

Our Lord was not ashamed to use the word "little". He used it again and again; and St. Thérèse merely follows him. So far from being ashamed to use it, he tells us explicitly that only those who are little can understand the secrets of the kingdom of heaven; that it is through the Father's infinite wisdom that those secrets remain hidden from those who put their trust in their own wisdom and prudence. *I confess to thee, O*

*Father, Lord of Heaven and earth, because thou hast hid these things
from the wise and prudent, and hast revealed them to little ones. Yea,
Father: for so hath it seemed good in thy sight.*[1] On another occasion he rebukes his disciples for keeping little children away
from him because, he says, the kingdom of heaven is for those
who are childlike: *Suffer the little children to come unto me, and
forbid them not; for of such is the kingdom of God. Amen I say to
you: whosoever shall not receive the kingdom of God as a little child
shall not enter into it.*[2] But most striking of all is the scene in
which he tells his apostles that unless they are converted from
all the world's false ideas of greatness, and become as little children, not even they can enter the kingdom of heaven. Then
he explains quite plainly what it is that his apostles must learn
from little children; it is their humility, their "littleness". *Amen
I say to you, unless you be converted and become as little children,
you shall not enter into the kingdom of heaven. Whosoever therefore
shall humble himself as this little child, he is the greater in the kingdom of heaven.*[3]

All the strength and power of those who follow the Little
Way lie in their littleness and humility, which to St. Thérèse
are one and the same thing. "Holiness does not consist in one
exercise or another, but in a disposition of the heart which
renders us humble and little in the hands of God."[4] "To reach
heaven I need not become great; on the contrary. I must remain
little, I must become even smaller than I am."[5] This same truth
she puts in a letter to her sister Céline: "One must be very little to draw near to Jesus! O how few are the souls who desire

[1] Mt 11:25–26.
[2] Mk 10:14–15.
[3] Mt 18:3–4.
[4] *Spirit of St. Thérèse*, comp. by the Carmelites of Lisieux (Burns and Oates),
p. 179.
[5] *Autobiography*, p. 152.

to be little and unknown!"[6] Therefore it is with perfect logic that she says: "What pleases God is to see me love my littleness."[7] Her love of humility is intense. On the day of her profession she bore next her heart a slip of paper on which were written these words: "O Jesus, grant that no one may think of me, that I may be forgotten and trodden underfoot as a grain of sand."[8] And towards the end of her life she prays: "I desire to humble myself in all sincerity, and to submit my will to that of my Sisters without ever contradicting them and without questioning whether they have the right to command."[9]

Does St. Thérèse exaggerate? We have already seen that the Gospels are her daily nourishment, and to St. Thérèse the Gospels were the Manual of Divine Humility. As she meditated on the Gospels, the Holy Spirit revealed to her secrets hidden from the wise and prudent. Our attention is specially drawn to this by the Holy See: "Above all she nourished heart and soul with the inspired Word of God on which she meditated assiduously, and the Spirit of Truth taught her what he hides as a rule from the wise and prudent and reveals to little ones."[10] St. Thérèse tells us herself how this came about.

Sometimes, when I read books in which perfection is put before us with the goal obstructed by a thousand obstacles, my poor head is quickly fatigued. I close the learned treatise which tires my brain and dries up my heart and I turn to the Sacred Scriptures. Then all becomes clear—a single word opens out new vistas, perfection appears easy, and I see it is enough to acknowledge one's nothingness and surrender oneself like a child into God's arms. Leaving to great

[6] Ibid., p. 343.
[7] Ibid., p. 360.
[8] Ibid., p. 136.
[9] Ibid., p. 453.
[10] Pope Pius XI, Homily at the Canonization.

and lofty minds the beautiful books which I cannot understand, still less put into practice, I rejoice in my littleness
because "only little children and those who are like them
shall be admitted to the Heavenly Banquet."[11]

As soon as I open the Gospels, I breathe the fragrance of
the life of Jesus and I know which way to run. It is not to
the highest place but to the lowest that I hasten. Leaving
the Pharisee to go forward, I repeat with all confidence the
humble prayer of the publican.[12]

For me, I find nothing in books with the exception of the
Gospels. That book suffices me. I hear with delight the
words of Jesus, in which He tells me all I have to do: *Learn
of Me, because I am meek and humble of heart.* That gives me
peace according to His promise: *And you shall find rest to
your soul.*[13]

It is no exaggeration, then, to say that to St. Thérèse the
Gospels were, above all, the Manual of Divine Humility. With
the Saint as our guide we will consider them and see how
entirely true this is.

It is in the setting of humility that the Incarnation is ush-
ered in. The Angel Gabriel is sent, not to Rome, the politi-
cal centre of the world, nor to Athens, the seat of learning,
nor to Jerusalem, the heart of the Jewish religion, but to
Nazareth, an unknown town hidden in the silence of the
Galilean hills. And in this humble town it was to the hum-
blest of its members that the Angel Gabriel came, for it was
the humility of Mary that drew God to choose her for his
Mother. We learn this from Our Lady's lips: *My spirit hath
rejoiced in God my Saviour. Because he hath regarded the humility*

[11] *Autobiography*, p. 372.
[12] Ibid., p. 194.
[13] *Novissima verba*, comp. by the Carmelites of Lisieux (Burns and Oates),
p. 4.

*of his handmaid. . . . He hath put down the mighty from their seat,
and hath exalted the humble.*[14]

When he was born, it was in the most humble setting. *And
she brought forth her firstborn son, and wrapped him up in swaddling
clothes, and laid him in a manger: because there was no room for them
in the inn.*[15] Thus took place the greatest event in the history
of the human race. For thirty years at Nazareth the Son of
God, unhurried and undisturbed, led the life of a village car-
penter, though the weight of the world's redemption lay upon
his shoulders. For thirty years Nazareth held this secret in its
heart, and none but Mary and Joseph knew the treasure hidden there.

When Our Lord leaves Nazareth for his public ministry the
blessedness of humility is the subject with which he opens his
first great sermon to the multitude which has gathered round
him. *Blessed are the poor in spirit: for theirs is the kingdom of heaven.
Blessed are the meek: for they shall possess the land.*[16] And when
he would teach his disciples the lesson which, above all others, he would have his followers learn from him, it is not to
his miracles nor to his doctrine, profound though it is, that he
directs their attention: it is to his humility. *Learn of me, because
I am meek and humble of heart: and you shall find rest to your souls.*[17]

In sharp contrast with the humility of Jesus was the pride
and self-satisfaction of the religious leaders of his time, the
scribes and Pharisees. Twice Our Lord condemns it. On the
first occasion, he is sitting at meat with them, and he gently
rebukes them for desiring to be first and to receive homage
from men. He tells them not to seek the foremost place, lest
a more honourable guest than they should arrive, and they, in

[14] Lk 1:47-52.
[15] Lk 2:7.
[16] Mt 5:3–4.
[17] Mt 11:29.

consequence, should have with shame to take the lowest place. *Because everyone that exalteth himself shall be humbled: and he that humbleth himself shall be exalted.*[18]

The second occasion is the last day in the Temple. Our Lord has made his appeal to the leaders of the Jews, and they have rejected it completely; and the reason for their rejection is their pride. Now, in the presence of his friends and his enemies, in the presence of the Pharisees themselves, before all the people, Our Lord condemns the scribes and Pharisees with unparalleled vehemence. In the Sermon on the Mount he opened with the blessedness of humility; now he opens with an indictment of pride. *The scribes and the Pharisees have sitten on the chair of Moses. All things therefore whatsoever they shall say to you, observe and do: but according to their works do ye not. For they say, and do not.... They love the first places at feasts, and the first chairs in the synagogues.... But...he that is the greatest among you shall be your servant. And whosoever shall exalt himself shall be humbled: and he that shall humble himself shall be exalted.*[19]

The subtleness of pride was pointed out by Our Lord in the parable of the Pharisee and the publican. In the person of the Pharisee Our Lord indicates the results of spiritual pride. It makes him stop short in himself and breeds scorn and criticism of his fellow-men. On the other hand, the humble and contrite prayer of the publican opens his soul to God, who can then lavish his grace upon him and use him for his own glory. The parable closes with the reiterated warning: *Everyone that exalteth himself shall be humbled: and he that humbleth himself shall be exalted.*[20]

We shall see with what earnestness he repeatedly tries to teach his own apostles the necessity of humility. If humility

[18] Lk 14:11.
[19] Mt 23:2–12.
[20] Lk 18:14.

was necessary for the scribes and Pharisees, much more was
it necessary for his own chosen band. The astonishing thing
is that although they had Our Lord's example always with
them, the apostles seem to have been unable to understand this
virtue. The first occasion was when they stood silent before
Our Lord, unable for very shame to tell him that they had been
arguing about which among them should be greatest. The
Divine Master makes his lesson most abundantly clear. First
he declares: *If any man desire to be first, he shall be the last of all
and the minister of all.*[21] Then seeing a child nearby and calling
him into their midst, he tells them that unless they are converted from all their false ideas of greatness and become as little children, so far from being first or second in his kingdom,
they will not even enter it! Finally he shows them where true
greatness lies. *Whosoever therefore shall humble himself as this little child, he is the greater in the kingdom of heaven.*[22]

The simplicity of this lesson is such that one wonders how
the apostles could have failed to understand it. Yet at the very
end of his public ministry the same question arises again. Two
of his apostles, James and John, come to him with a request:
*Master, we desire that whatsoever we shall ask, thou wouldst do it for
us.* A perfect example of a completely wrong prayer, an
attempt to twist the Divine Will to theirs. Our Lord does not
rebuke them. With all their blindness he loves them. He
merely asks: *What would you that I should do for you?* They
answer: *Grant us that we may sit, one on thy right hand, and the
other on thy left hand in thy glory.* Again Jesus does not rebuke
them. He merely tells them that they know not what they ask
and that it is not his to give. At this point there comes a very
human touch. *And the ten hearing it began to be much displeased
at James and John.* Why? Because they understood what James

[21] Mk 9:34.
[22] Mt 18:4.

and John had failed to grasp? We shall see that this was not so. It was rather because they wanted, like James and John, to be first or second. Once more Jesus gathers them round him and, using this time the very same words as before, tries to teach them humility, only this time by directing their attention to his own example. *Whosoever will be first among you shall be the servant of all. For the Son of man also is not come to be ministered unto: but to minister and to give his life a redemption for many.*[23]

Surely the twelve have learned their lesson. But no, the same trouble occurs again—in the Upper Room on the evening of his Passion and, incredible as it seems, at the supper-table, immediately after the first Mass. *And there was also a strife amongst them, which of them should seem to be the greater. Once again Our Lord repeats his lesson: He that is the greater among you, let him become as the younger: and he that is the leader, as he that serveth.... But I am in the midst of you, as he that serveth.*[24]

Yet this time he goes further; he himself gives them an example. *He riseth from supper and layeth aside his garments and, having taken a towel, girded himself. After that, he putteth water into a basin, and began to wash the feet of the disciples, and to wipe them with the towel wherewith he was girded.... Then after he had washed their feet, and taken his garments, being set down again, he said to them: Know you what I have done to you? You call me Master and Lord. And you say well, for so I am. If then I being your Lord and Master, have washed your feet, you also ought to wash one another's feet. For I have given you an example, that as I have done to you, so you do also.*[25] The twelve never forgot this scene, and the Church has preserved its memory for all time in the washing of the feet on Maundy Thursday.

His own example of humility, given to his disciples in the

[23] Mk 10:35–45.
[24] Lk 22:24–27.
[25] Jn 13:4–15.

Upper Room, was but the prelude to the supreme manifestation of it in his acceptance of the Cross, which has become
the standard borne by all who follow him. From the Upper
Room to Calvary, it was one series of humiliations. The men
who took him prisoner in Gethsemane *mocked him and struck
him. And they blindfolded him and smote his face.*[26]

He is taken before the Sanhedrin and is condemned as
guilty of death. Again the mocking is repeated, but this time
they not only strike the Sacred Face, they also spit upon it.
And this was done by the religious leaders of the day. *Then
did they spit in his face, and buffeted him. And others struck his face
with the palms of their hands.*[27] He is taken before Pilate, his
Sacred Body is torn by the scourgings, and then, while he is
left waiting to be taken to Calvary, he is publicly mocked once
more by the soldiers. *And stripping him they put a scarlet cloak
about him. And plaiting a crown of thorns, they put it upon his head,
and a reed in his right hand. And bowing the knee before him, they
mocked him, saying: Hail, King of the Jews.*[28]

The soldiers take him to Calvary. He is nailed to the Cross
and dies between two criminals on the public scaffold. His
body is taken down and buried in a grave. So closes the story
of the humiliation of the Son of God. With Our Lord's example before us, we dare not call St. Thérèse's love of humility
exaggerated or unpractical.

Why did the Father allow his Son to be so humiliated in
his Passion? Why did he permit his creatures to strike and spit
upon his Sacred Face? Because without humility there can be
no salvation; we must be brought to realize this no matter what
the cost. The root of all sin is pride. Pride, the desire to be as
gods, was the motive of that disobedience which caused the

[26] Lk 22:63–64.
[27] Mt 26:67.
[28] Mt 27:28–29.

Fall and the consequent flood of sin and misery. Pride being the cause of sin and of the loss of heaven, humility will be the key to salvation and to the regaining of the kingdom of heaven, but since man's disobedience was an offence against God, only God could make true reparation; therefore the key to the kingdom of heaven is the humility of the Son of God.

By his act of humble obedience on the Cross, Our Lord overcame sin and its cause, restoring all that had been lost. By this willing acceptance of a humiliating death, he overcame death and the devil. He was obedient unto death, death on a Cross, *that, through death, he might destroy him who had the empire of death, that is to say, the devil.*[29]

Unless you be converted and become as little children you shall not enter into the kingdom of heaven. We see now why, in spite of Our Lord's insistence on humility, the apostles found it so very hard to learn the lesson. The secret lies in the word "converted". Pride being the cause of all sin, to practise humility meant for the apostles the conversion of their nature at the point where it was most badly damaged and most warped by original sin.

What was hard for the apostles will not be easy for us. It is the most difficult thing in the world to become humble. It must be so, for to practise humility is to cut at the very roots of sin; it is to undo the results of the devil's supreme achievement, the Fall. He will do anything to stop our being humble, and he is very subtle. His great aim is to deceive us so that we do not see things as they really are. First he blinds us to the fact that pride is the greatest of all sins. He leads us to think that other sins are more important, and so the most deadly one slips through unnoticed. Secondly, when we do realize the importance of pride in general, he blinds us to the reality of

---

[29] Heb 2:14.

pride in our own case. Finally, even when we do recognize our own pride, he so plays upon our self-love that we cannot face the conversion necessary—that conversion which alone can deliver us out of the bonds of pride into the freedom of humility.

Humility is the logical putting into practice of the teaching of the Gospels, to which Thérèse unerringly leads us back. They are, above all else, the Manual of Divine Humility, and it was from these that she drew the inspiration of her prayer for humility, with which we will close this chapter:

O Jesus, when Thou wast a wayfarer upon earth, Thou didst say: *Learn of Me because I am meek and humble of heart and you shall find rest to your souls.* O Almighty King of Heaven! My soul indeed finds rest in seeing Thee thus condescend to wash the feet of Thy Apostles—*having taken the form of a slave.* I recall the words Thou didst utter to teach me the practice of humility: *I have given you an example, that as I have done to you, so do you also. The servant is not greater than his Lord. . . . If you know these things, you shall be blessed if you do them.* I understand, dear Lord, these words which come from Thy meek and humble heart, and I wish to put them into practice with the help of Thy grace.

I desire to humble myself in all sincerity, and to submit my will to that of my Sisters, without ever contradicting them, and without questioning whether they have the right to command. No one, O my Beloved, had that right over Thee, and yet Thou didst obey not only the Blessed Virgin and St. Joseph but even Thy executioners. And now, in the Holy Eucharist, I see Thee complete in Thy self-abasement. O Divine King of Glory, with wondrous humility Thou dost submit Thyself to all Thy priests, without any distinction between those who love Thee and those who, alas, are lukewarm or cold in Thy service. They may advance or delay the hour of the Holy

Sacrifice: Thou art always ready to come down from Heaven at their call.

O my Beloved, under the white Eucharistic veil thou dost indeed appear to me meek and humble of heart! To teach me humility, Thou canst not further abase Thyself, and so I wish to respond to Thy Love by putting myself in the lowest place, by sharing Thy humiliations, so that I may have part with Thee in the kingdom of Heaven.

I implore Thee, dear Jesus, to send me a humiliation whensoever I try to set myself above others. Thou knowest my weakness. Each morning I resolve to be humble, and in the evening I recognize that I have often been guilty of pride. The sight of these faults tempts me to discouragement: yet I know that discouragement is itself a form of pride. I wish therefore, O my God, to build all my trust upon Thee. As Thou canst do all things, deign to implant in my soul this virtue which I desire: and to obtain it from Thy infinite mercy, I will often say to Thee: Jesus, meek and humble of heart, make my heart like unto Thine.[30]

---

[30] *Autobiography*, pp. 453–54.

VI

HUMILITY (2)

IN THE PRECEDING CHAPTER we have seen the necessity of humility as understood by St. Thérèse; now we will consider her conception of its nature.

> Think of your Thérèse during this month of the Infant Jesus, and beg of Him that she may always remain a very little child. I shall offer the same prayer for you, because I know your desires and that humility is your favourite virtue. Which of us will be the more fervent? She who is the more humble, the more closely united to Jesus, and the more faithful in making love the mainspring of every action. We must not let slip one single occasion of sacrifice.[1]

So wrote Thérèse to her sister Léonie two years before her death. In these words she sets out her view on the place humility should have in our spiritual life. To her it is a virtue to be embraced primarily as a means to union with Our Blessed Lord, a virtue demanding sacrifice and exercised in the ordinary duties of our daily life.

With St. Thérèse humility is truth. "To me," she says, "it seems that humility is truth. I do not know whether I am humble, but I do know that I see the truth in all things."[2] We are truly humble only when we see ourselves as God sees us.

[1] *Autobiography*, p. 363.
[2] Ibid., p. 297.

This is a great grace, but, at the same time, it is a thing from which we shrink. We must bring ourselves to admit with sincerity: "I am really only what I am in His eyes."[3]

This loyalty to truth St. Thérèse pressed home in every detail of her life. In the *Autobiography* she writes that when she was quite a little girl, on hearing an action insincerely, as she thought, commended, she said to herself: "I should not have done that. We must always speak the truth."[4] In recording this incident, long years afterward, when she was Novice Mistress and so in a position of authority, she adds: "And now I always speak it. It gives me a great deal of trouble, of course, but let nobody come to me if she does not want to be told the truth."[5]

She had no use for fancies in her spirituality. When one of the Sisters suggested that beautiful angels, all robed in white, with joyful, shining faces, would bear her soul to heaven, the Saint tersely said: "Fancies like these do not help me; my soul can feed only upon truth."[6]

Again she says: "Yes, it does seem to me that I am humble. God shows me the truth and I see clearly that everything comes from Him."[7]

A little after half-past two on the day she died—she died soon after seven o'clock—the Mother Prioress said to her: "My child, you are quite ready to appear before God because you have always understood the virtue of humility." To this St. Thérèse replied faintly: "Yes, I feel that my soul has never sought anything but the truth."[8] These were almost her exact words.

[3] Ibid., p. 300.

[4] Ibid., p. 324.

[5] Ibid.

[6] Ibid., p. 327.

[7] *Novissima verba*, comp. by the Carmelites of Lisieux (Burns and Oates), p. 107.

[8] *Autobiography*, p. 239.

To see the truth in all things, to see ourselves and all around us as Our Lord does, is one of the greatest needs in our lives.

This detaches us from our own narrow point of view, enables us to judge calmly and speak without fear of human respect. This grace was St. Thérèse's supreme desire, and she prayed for it earnestly. "O my God, make me to see things as they really are, that I may not be deceived by any illusion. Thou knowest, O my God, that I seek the truth." [9]

When, with the help of grace, we begin to see things as they really are, the first thing we learn is that God is everything and that, apart from him, we are nothing. *Without me you can do nothing.*[10]

St. Thérèse had an overwhelming sense of her nothingness apart from Our Lord. It appears constantly in her writings. For her, being little meant admitting what she really was. "To be a little child means to recognize our nothingness, to look for everything from God, as a little child looks for everything from its father." [11] It is difficult to accept this truth. However well we may recognize it in theory, in practice we act as if we were convinced of our own power to deal with situations, we trust too readily in the strength of our own right arm. An old and wise priest once made this profound remark: "We all think we know our powers, some of us say we know our faults; none of us knows his nothingness, and that's the only thing that matters." The power of Our Lord's lesson to his apostles on humility is precisely this, that it shows us our dependence on Almighty God by bringing it home to us through the dependence of a little child, a dependence which everyone sees at once to be absolute and complete. It is the mission of St.

---

[9] *Spirit of St. Thérèse*, comp. by the Carmelites of Lisieux (Burns and Oates), p. 120.

[10] Jn 15:5.

[11] *Autobiography*, p. 295.

Thérèse to recall to us this simple Gospel lesson. "It is to God alone that all worth must be attributed. There is nothing of value in my little nothingness." [12] She used to sign her letters to Mother Agnes "Votre tout petit néant." There is nothing superficial here; St. Thérèse meant it, and it is pure Scripture: *My substance is as nothing before thee.* [13]

It is interesting to follow the progress of her thought on her own nothingness.

"O Brother, how little known is the Merciful Love of the Heart of Jesus. It is true that to enjoy that treasure we must humble ourselves, must confess our nothingness; and here is where many a soul draws back." [14]

Yet she does not look at her nothingness apart from her possession of Our Lord. "Marie, though you are nothing, do not forget that Jesus is all. You have only to lose your nothingness in that Infinite All and thenceforth to think only of that All who alone is worthy of your love." [15]

Our Lord chose his apostles for the most exalted vocation, to handle things that were beyond all human comprehension. In training them for this vocation, he stressed again and again their dependence upon him. The miraculous draught of fishes is one occasion of this. The apostles had toiled all night and had taken nothing; then at Jesus' word they once more let down the net, and it was filled with fish. Night and nothing—such are our efforts without Our Lord. The lesson of this miracle was understood by St. Thérèse. She says:

> The Apostles laboured without Him. They toiled the whole night and caught no fish. Their labours were not unacceptable to Him, but He wished to prove that He is

[12] *Novissima verba*, p. 123.
[13] Ps 38:6.
[14] *Autobiography*, p. 373.
[15] Ibid., p. 367.

the Giver of all things. He asked for an act of humility. St. Peter, avowing his helplessness, cried out: *Lord, we have laboured all night and taken nothing.* The heart of Jesus was deeply touched by his confession. If the apostles had caught some small fish, perhaps Jesus would not have wrought a miracle. But they had caught nothing. So, through the power of God, the net was filled with great fishes. Such is Our Lord's way. He gives as God, with divine generosity, but He insists on humility of heart.[16]

To know ourselves as we really are is to recognize that we are a strange mixture of good and bad. We have talents and we have weaknesses. It is not humility to say that we can do nothing, for each of us is endowed with certain gifts, given us by Almighty God in order that we may fulfil the purpose for which he has placed us in this world—a purpose which we, and we alone, can fulfil. To realize this, we must become as little children.

> To be little is not to attribute to oneself the virtues one practises, believing oneself capable of something, but to recognize that God puts the treasure of virtue into the hands of His little children, to serve Him when there is need of it, but it is always the treasure which belongs to God Himself.[17]

St. Thérèse was a realist; she knew that God had given her great gifts and graces, yet never for one moment did she forget that they were gifts, to be used solely for him. She never took credit to herself for anything. One day the Mother Prioress brought her a little sheaf of corn. St. Thérèse took an ear of corn which was so laden with grain that it bent upon its stalk. After looking at it for some time, she said to the

16 Ibid., pp. 346–47.
17 Ibid., p. 295.

Mother Prioress: "That ear of corn, dear Mother, is the image of my soul which God has loaded with graces for me and many others; and it is my earnest desire to bend beneath the weight of His gifts, acknowledging that all comes from Him." [18] As her life drew to its close, and some of the Sisters began to realize her virtues, she was more than ever insistent that they came solely from God. "No, I am not a Saint. I have never performed the works of the Saints. I am just a little soul whom God has overwhelmed with His grace. You will see in heaven that all I say is the truth." [19] With almost passionate earnestness, she begs those around her not to attribute anything to herself. One of the Sisters spoke of the beauty of her soul. St. Thérèse replied quickly: "What beauty? I do not at all see my beauty. I see only the graces which I have received from God." [20] Again: "I have never had patience, not for a single minute. It is not mine. You are all mistaken." [21]

Our gifts may be our greatest temptation. Only those who are little children—that is to say, conscious from beginning to end of their utter nothingness—can escape the snare. We must become children again if we have lost this realization of our dependence upon God and, like children, keep our hand tightly in his. *Unless you be converted and become as little children, you shall not enter into the kingdom of heaven.* Whatever our talents, they bear fruit only when used in partnership with Our Lord, from whom they come; alone, we have nothing in which to glory. *What hast thou that thou hast not received? And if thou hast received, why dost thou glory, as though thou hadst not received it?* [22] One of the surest means of testing ourselves is to

[18] Ibid., p. 229.
[19] *Novissima verba*, p. 127.
[20] Ibid., p. 128.
[21] Ibid., p. 138.
[22] 1 Cor 4:7.

examine our attitude towards our daily faults and imperfections. Most of us refuse to face these imperfections squarely,
yet, as St. Thérèse points out, "the Heart of Jesus is more
grieved by the countless little imperfections of His friends than
by the faults, however grave, that His enemies commit." [23]

Humility is seeing things as they really are and accepting
them without bitterness. It enables us to use our gifts safely,
to the glory of God and not for our own aggrandizement.
Also, it enables us to learn from our faults our complete
dependence upon God, so that we surrender ourselves,
together with those faults, into the arms of Our Lord and let
him transform them into means of union with him. In this
way, so far from being impatient or discouraged, we learn to
welcome the knowledge of them.

"We must never be discouraged by our faults," [24] says St.
Thérèse. And not only this, but again she says: "I am happy
to see how imperfect I am." [25] And again she gives us her reason: it is because her failings teach her her weakness. "It
happens to me often that I fail thus, but I am never astonished
at it. . . . I say to myself: 'I am back at the first step, as before';
but this I say in great peace, without sadness; it is so good to
feel oneself to be little and weak." [26] "My weakness is still very
great. Every day some new and wholesome experience brings
this home more clearly." [27] "The remembrance of my faults
humbles me, and helps me never to rely on my own strength,
which is mere weakness." [28] The consciousness of her weakness throws her more completely into the arms of Our Lord.

[23] *Autobiography*, p. 373.
[24] *Novissima verba*, p. 119.
[25] Ibid., p. 91.
[26] Ibid., p. 37.
[27] *Autobiography*, p. 367.
[28] Ibid., p. 371.

"Of course we should like never to fall. What an illusion! What does it matter if I fall every moment? In that way I realize my weakness, and in that I find great gain. My God, You see what I am if You do not hold me in Your arms."[29]

True humility, therefore, is a most active thing, and humility in action is the removing, through surrender to grace, of all these faults and failings, so that, where pride and self-love have hitherto dominated, the love of Our Lord may reign instead.

"When one accepts with sweetness the humiliation of having fallen into some imperfection, the grace of God returns at once."[30] "All we have to do is to humble ourselves, to bear with meekness our imperfections. Herein lies for us true holiness."[31] "Jesus can grant me the grace never to offend Him any more, or rather never to commit any faults but those which do not offend Him or give Him pain, faults which serve to humble me and strengthen my love."[32] "It is true I am not always faithful, but I never lose courage. I leave myself in the arms of Our Lord. He teaches me to draw profit from everything, from the good and from the bad which He finds in me."[33]

Now we understand why St. Thérèse says: "It does not worry me to find that I am weakness itself. In this I glory; and I expect every day to discover new imperfections in me; and I acknowledge that these lights on my own nothingness do me more good than lights on matters of faith."[34]

At first this sounds startling. Yet it is true; for where there is pride the light of faith cannot penetrate. Lights on the faith

<hr>

[29] Ibid., p. 336.
[30] *Novissima verba*, p. 165.
[31] *Autobiography*, p. 303.
[32] Ibid., p. 354.
[33] Ibid., p. 345.
[34] Ibid., p. 170.

may indeed minister to spiritual pride, but the humble placing of one's infirmities in the hands of Jesus is a sure road to
sanctity. Like St. Thérèse we must learn to say: "Jesus does
everything in me. I just remain little and weak." [35] Only then
can we say with truth: "My very weakness makes me strong." [36]
"It is Jesus who takes upon Himself to fill our souls according as we rid them of imperfections." [37]

In all of this we notice how truly Pauline is St. Thérèse's
teaching. *My grace is sufficient for thee: for power is made perfect in
infirmity. Gladly therefore will I glory in my infirmities, that the power
of Christ may dwell in me. For which cause I please myself in my
infirmities . . . . For when I am weak, then am I powerful.* [38] *I can do
all things in him who strengtheneth me.* [39]

St. Thérèse calls us back to this truth. "I pray that Jesus may
take possession of all my powers, all my faculties, that henceforth my actions may be solely divine, inspired and directed
by His Holy Spirit of Love." [40]

This aspiration of St. Thérèse's may well become our own
prayer, but always we must remember that it is by the
sanctification of our weaknesses that this sublime prayer finds
its fulfilment; and this is just one of those secrets which are
hidden from the wise and prudent and revealed only to little
ones.

---

[35] August Pierre Laveille, *St. Thérèse de l'Enfant Jésus* (Clonmore and Reynolds), p. 307.

[36] *Autobiography*, p. 352.

[37] Ibid., p. 297.

[38] 2 Cor 12:9–10.

[39] Phil 4:13.

[40] *Autobiography*, p. 318.

VII

HUMILITY (3)

I F WE ARE TO FOLLOW St. Thérèse's Little Way of Spiritual
Childhood we must be humble. In order to teach us this
she takes us to the Gospels and lights up for us anew the words
of Our Lord: *Whosoever therefore shall humble himself as this little
child, he is the greater in the kingdom of heaven.*[1] Now she is to
lead us further and to show us how humility can be fashioned
only through humiliation. In order to do this she once again
takes us to the Gospels, this time to teach us the secret of the
Holy Face.

It is well known that from her earliest days St. Thérèse had
a special devotion to the Holy Child, and that on her entrance
into Carmel she was providentially given the name of
"Thérèse of the Child Jesus"; it is not so widely known that
later on there was added to that name the further title "and
of the Holy Face", on account of her particular devotion to
the humiliation of the Passion. To St. Thérèse of the Child
Jesus and of the Holy Face we now turn to learn what inspired
this second devotion.

"I know that by humiliation alone can Saints be made."[2]
Here St. Thérèse takes us right into the secret of sanctity. A
readiness to acknowledge our faults is absolutely essential, but

[1] Mt 18:4.
[2] *Autobiography*, p. 335.

in order to remove our faults we must know them, and in order to know them we must be told them, either directly by Almighty God or by our fellow-men: we must submit to the humiliation of being told.

Why do we find this so difficult? Surely because it strikes at our self-love. It wounds our self-esteem because, in our fallen state, our own individual excellence is our most treasured fancy. Unwillingness to be told our faults is a sure symptom of that malady deepset in every one of us.

St. Thérèse reminds us that we must do all in our power to eradicate it and that a willing response to correction, or acceptance of what we really are, is a mark of holiness: in fact we can measure our sanctity by our willingness to be told our faults.

The road of humiliation was the path which St. Thérèse trod from the moment of her entrance into Carmel.

To begin with... Our Lord permitted that the Mother Prioress, Mother Marie Gonzague, sometimes unconsciously, should treat me with much severity. She never met me without finding fault, and I remember on one occasion when I had left a cobweb in the cloister, she said to me before the whole community: "It is easy to see that our cloisters are swept by a child of fifteen! It is disgraceful! Go and sweep that cobweb away and be more careful in future." On the rare occasions when I went to her for spiritual direction, she seemed to scold me nearly all the time, and what troubled me more than anything was that I did not understand how to correct my faults, my slow ways for instance and my want of thoroughness.... Yet, dear Mother, I thank God for having provided me with so sound and valuable a training; it was a priceless grace. What should I have become if, as the world outside believed, I had been made the pet of the community? Instead of seeing Our Lord in the person of my superior, I might have consid-

ered only the creature, and my heart, so carefully guarded
in the world, would have been ensnared by human affection in the cloister. Happily I was preserved from such a
disaster.[3]

Writing for Mother Gonzague herself she thanked her for
the humiliations she had imposed.

I thank you, Mother, for not having spared me: Jesus knew
that His Little Flower was too weak to take root without
the life-giving waters of humiliation, and it is to you that
she owes that inestimable blessing. For some months the
Divine Master has completely changed His method of cul-
tivation. Finding, no doubt, that His Little Flower has been
sufficiently watered, He allows her to grow up under the
warm rays of a brilliant sun. He only smiles upon her now
and it is you, dear Reverend Mother, who mirror His smile
to me. The bright sunlight, far from withering her petals,
fosters their growth in a marvellous way. Deep in her heart
she treasures those precious drops of dew—the humiliations
of other days—and they remind her always how frail she
is. Were all creatures to draw near and pour out their
flattery, no vain satisfaction would mingle with her joyful
realization that in God's eyes she is a poor worthless thing
and nothing more.... I feel that I have nothing now to fear
from praise, and can listen to it unmoved, attributing to
God all that is good in me. If it pleases Him to make me
appear better than I am, that does not concern me; He can
act as He will.[4]

When she wrote those lines St. Thérèse had reached a high
degree of perfection. She was fully conscious of her worth-
lessness apart from God and willing to admit it. The acceptance of humiliation was one of the ways in which she did so.

[3] Ibid., pp. 122–23.
[4] Ibid., p. 150.

"When misunderstood and judged unfavourably, what benefit do we derive from defending ourselves? Leave things as they are and say nothing. It is good to allow ourselves to be judged anyhow, rightly or wrongly." [5] She prefers to be rebuked unjustly in order that she may have something to offer to God. "I prefer to be rebuked unjustly because, having nothing to reproach myself with, I offer gladly this little injustice to God. Then, humbling myself, I think how easily I might have deserved the reproach." [6] Finally she turns it all into an instrument for the conversion of sinners. "Through compassion for sinners, to obtain their conversion, I beseech Thee, O my God, to permit that I may be well rebuked by the souls who are around me." [7]

But God can bring our faults home to us directly by a sudden flash of interior light, giving us a deeper realization of the sort of person we really are; if taken the right way this is one of the greatest graces God can give us. "The Almighty has done great things for me, and the *greatest* is to show me my littleness and my helplessness for any good." [8]

It is by such means that Our Lord fashions and perfects those through whom he desires to draw others. "When Our Lord lavishes His gifts on a soul in order to draw yet other souls to Him, He humbles it inwardly, gently compelling it to recognize its utter nothingness and His almighty power." [9] Thus does St. Thérèse show us the purpose of humiliation. It frees the soul from pride and self-love so that it becomes a channel through which the love of Our Lord can pass to others.

[5] Ibid., p. 312.
[6] Ibid., p. 311.
[7] Ibid., p. 312.
[8] Ibid., p. 154.
[9] Ibid., p. 344.

It is often as difficult to correct as to be corrected, especially if we are to do it in a really impartial and supernatural way; the natural man in us leaps so readily to criticize, and few things do so much harm as a reproof given through personal feelings or prejudice. It is difficult enough to take a reproof when it is given solely from the motive of supernatural charity: given from partly natural motives it may be quite unbearable.

St. Thérèse knew this. She tells us that when a reproof is given, it should involve pain for the one who gives it, no less than for the one who receives it.

> I would prefer to receive a thousand reproofs rather than inflict one, yet I feel it necessary that the task should cause me some pain, for if I spoke through natural impulse only, the soul in fault would not understand that she was in the wrong, and would simply think: "The Sister in charge of me is annoyed about something, and vents her displeasure on me, although I am full of the best intentions." [10]

Again she says: "Before a reproof [to a novice] bears fruit, it must cost something and be free from the least trace of passion." [11]

It was not always so with St. Thérèse. She tells us how she had to learn this through her own experience.

> Formerly, when I saw a Sister doing something I did not like and seemingly contrary to our rule, I used to think how glad I should be if I could only warn her, and point out her mistake. But since the burden of Novice-Mistress has been laid upon me and it has become my duty to find fault, my ideas have undergone a change. Now when I see something wrong I heave a sigh of relief. I thank God that the

[10] Ibid., p. 176.
[11] Ibid., p. 324.

guilty one is not a novice, and that it is not my business to correct her; then I do all I can to make excuses for her, and to credit her with the good intentions which she no doubt possesses.[12]

What wrought that change? Only those who understand the difficulty yet necessity of accepting humiliation can safely correct others. We must ourselves be trained in the willing acceptance of humiliation. There are various ways in which this willingness can be shown. The simplest and most obvious way is to accept with complete willingness every humiliation which comes to us from authority; but the best and surest way is to ask Our Lord to train us himself by showing us our faults in order to free us from self-love. She gives us the words with which we may do this: "Oh, that I might be humiliated to see if I really have humility of heart!"[13] "I implore Thee, Jesus, to send me a humiliation whenever I try to set myself above others."[14]

What led St. Thérèse to understand so clearly the necessity and the blessedness of humiliation? What was it that led her to say: "I know that by humiliation alone can Saints be made"? It was surely contemplation of the Face of Our Lord in his Passion. In her own words: "The Little Flower gradually unfolded under the shadow of His Cross, having for refreshing dew His Tears and His Blood, and for its radiant sun His adorable Face."[15]

"For its radiant sun His adorable Face." Those words give us the clue to St. Thérèse's devotion to the Holy Face. How is it that the Holy Face, blindfolded, beaten, blood-stained,

---

[12] Ibid., p. 182.

[13] *Novissima verba*, comp. by the Carmelites of Lisieux (Burns and Oates), p. 107.

[14] *Autobiography*, p. 453.

[15] Ibid., p. 125.

and spat upon, is the radiant sun in whose warmth the soul expands and flowers? St. Thérèse explains this. She first learned the devotion from Mother Agnes. Speaking of her very first days in Carmel she says:

> Until then I had not appreciated the beauties of the Holy Face, and it was you, my little Mother, who unveiled them to me. Just as you had been the first to leave our home for Carmel, so you too were the first to penetrate the mysteries of love hidden in the Face of our Divine Spouse. Having discovered them you showed them to me—and I understood. More than ever did it come to me in what true glory consists. He whose *kingdom is not of this world* taught me that the only kingdom worth coveting is the grace of being "unknown and esteemed as naught", and the joy that comes from self-contempt. I wished that like the Face of Jesus, mine should be *as it were hidden and despised*, so that no one on earth should esteem me: I thirsted to suffer and to be forgotten.[16]

Here for the moment we will notice merely the two things which St. Thérèse specially mentions. First, the love of Our Lord who accepted such humiliation to teach us that this is the only way to heaven. Secondly, the response of her soul to that revelation. She would be like him, hidden and despised.

From that moment devotion to the Holy Face so took possession of her soul that she asked to have the title "and of the Holy Face" added to that of "the Child Jesus" which she already had. Her own sisters have said that it would be impossible to decide which was her greater devotion. We do know that from her earliest days in Carmel, devotion to the Holy Face played a very great part in determining her spirituality.

[16] Ibid.

Through all her nine years in Carmel she never wearied of it, and she had a picture of the Holy Face pinned to the curtain of her sick-bed, to be her support in the hour of her death. *Adjuvabit eam Deus vultu suo.*[17]

This devotion is rooted in the Scriptures. *The confusion of my face hath covered me.*[18] With those words the Psalmist foreshadows the humiliation of the Holy Face. In Isaiah the prophecy becomes more detailed. *I have given... my cheeks to them that plucked them: I have not turned away my face from them that rebuked me and spit upon me.*[19] When the same prophet gives us the supreme prophecy of the Passion of Our Lord, it is with a most striking description of the humiliation of the Holy Face that he opens it: *No beauty in him, nor comeliness... despised and the most abject of men, a man of sorrows, and acquainted with infirmity.*[20]

But that humiliation is not merely negative; it results in the conversion of many souls to God and in the triumph of the Divine Will. *He shall see a long-lived seed: and the will of the Lord shall be prosperous in his hand.*[21]

When we turn to the Gospels, we find the humiliation of the Holy Face recorded in all its horror. The first occasion is in the presence of the chief priests and the council; the second in the presence of the soldiers. Of the council we read: *Then did they spit in his face, and buffeted him. And others struck his face with the palms of their hands.*[22] *And some began to spit on him, and to cover his face, and to buffet him.*[23]

With the soldiers it is the same: *And spitting upon him, they took the reed and struck his head.*[24] *And they struck his head with a reed, and they did spit on him.*[25]

---

[17] Office of Our Lady.   [18] Ps 43:16.
[19] Is 1:6.   [20] Is 53:2–3.
[21] Is 53:10.   [22] Mt 26:67.
[23] Mk 14:65.   [24] Mt 27:30.
[25] Mk 15:19.

The climax of humiliation is reached when Pilate brings out Our Lord with his Sacred Face bleeding, bruised, and spat upon, and introduces him to the crowd with the words: *Behold the Man.*[26]

Why did Our Lord accept such humiliation? To bring home to us our pride for which this is the payment and, by paying this price, to show us how much he loves us. But he accepted humiliation not only in reparation for our pride, but also as an example to us. We must share his humiliation if we are to be his members. We shall accept humiliation willingly only when we realize that we are sharing it with him and that it is really Our Lord who is suffering it again, in and through us, and giving our acceptance a divine value. Only so shall we attain to that supernatural sense of the blessedness of humiliation which will detach us from self-love, so that he can truly live in us and carry on the work he began during the Passion.

St. Thérèse's devotion finds concise expression in the following lines:

> *Ta face est ma seule richesse:*
> *Je ne demande rien de plus:*
> *En elle me cachant sans cesse,*
> *Je te ressemblerai, Jésus.*
> *Laisse en moi la divine empreinte*
> *De tes traits remplis de douceurs,*
> *Et bientôt je deviendrai sainte:*
> *Vers toi j'attirerai les cœurs!* [27]

---

[26] Jn 19:5.

[27] "Thy Face, Lord, is my secret store:/ No more I have, I ask no more:/ Hidden continually there/ Thy inward likeness let me share./ Trace in my soul the prints divine/ Of all the sweetness that is thine—/ Sweetness, that soon shall make of me/ A Saint, to draw men's hearts to thee."—"A la Sainte Face", *Poems*. The translation of this, and of the other verses quoted in this chapter, is by Msgr. R. A. Knox.

Let us study those lines carefully.

> *Ta face est ma seule richesse:*
> *Je ne demande rien de plus.*

In these words St. Thérèse tells us that in the spiritual life the Holy Face is everything to her. She has already told us this: "The Little Flower ... unfolded ..., having for refreshing dew His Tears and His Blood, and for its radiant sun His adorable Face." [28]

In the natural order the sun is the source of light; in the warmth of its rays spring forth the beauties of the natural world. In the spiritual order the holy life of grace can blossom in the soul; for the divine Face is, to St. Thérèse, the sun under whose rays the humiliation alone can dispel pride with its spiritual darkness and death. Pride clouds our intellect, we do not know where to go nor how to get there, we stumble along helplessly in the dark. He who said: *I am the light of the world*, has shown us by his acceptance of humiliation how to dispel the darkness of our souls. *Domine, in lumine vultus tui ambulabunt.*[29] By imitating him she found true joy, that "joy which comes from self-contempt".[30] *Adimplebis me laetitia cum vultu tuo.*[31]

> *Oui, je te reconnais, même à travers tes larmes,*
> *Face de l'Eternel, je découvre tes charmes.*
>> *Que ton regard voilé*
>> *Mon cœur a consolé*
>> *Rappelle-toi.*[32]

---

[28] *Autobiography*, p. 125.

[29] Ps 88:16.

[30] *Autobiography*, p. 125.

[31] Ps 15:11.

[32] "Face of eternal God! At least these eyes,/ Even through thy tears, thy beauty recognize:/ How that veiled sight of thee/ Has soothed my misery,/ Remember still."—"Jésus, rappelle-toi", *Poems*.

She longs to share it all with him, to respond to Our Lord's love revealed in this mystery, to return love for love. "O Blessed Face, from Thy adorable lips we have heard Thy loving plaint: *I thirst.* Since we know that this thirst which consumes Thee is a thirst for love, to quench it we would wish to possess an infinite love. Dear Spouse of our souls, if we could love Thee with the love of all hearts, that love would be Thine.... Give us, Lord, that love."[33] The next few lines of the stanza tell us how she will respond.

> *En elle me cachant sans cesse,*
> *Je te ressemblerai, Jésus,*
> *Laisse en moi la divine empreinte*
> *De tes traits remplis de douceurs.*

She desires to be conformed to him, one with him, as it were hidden in him.

> *Ah! laisse-moi, Seigneur, me cacher en ta face;*
> *Là je n'entendrai plus du monde le vain bruit.*
> *Donne-moi ton amour, conserve-moi ta grâce,*
> *Rien que pour aujourd'hui.*[34]

St. Thérèse is but echoing the words of Scripture: *Abscondes eos in abscondito faciei tuae, a conturbatione hominum.*[35] We are *hidden with Christ in God,* as St. Paul says, but here we are to be conformed to him as he was on earth, to Our Lord humiliated; and to learn that, we must often meditate on the Holy Face. The fruit of such meditation is a complete detachment from the praise and blame of the world and a peace which

---

[33] *Autobiography,* p. 450.

[34] "Where shall I hide me, Lord, but in thy face,/ From the world's noisy striving far away?/ Grant me thy love, and keep me in thy grace,/ No thought beyond today."—"Mon chant d'aujourd'hui", *Poems.*

[35] Ps 30:20–21.

allows Our Lord to transform us more easily into himself. These lines of St. Thérèse's express it. In her prayer to the Holy Face, she prays for this: "O adorable Face of Jesus, sole beauty which ravishest my heart, vouchsafe to impress on my soul Thy divine likeness, so that it may not be possible for Thee to look at Thy spouse without beholding Thyself." [36] This peace does not lie in the feelings, but in a right relationship with Our Blessed Lord—union with him through a completely surrendered will—that rest of soul, in fact, which he promised to those who learn humility from him.

The last four lines of the stanza sum up her ideal.

> *Laisse en moi la divine empreinte*
> *De tes traits remplis de douceurs,*
> *Et bientôt je deviendrai sainte:*
> *Vers toi j'attirerai les cœurs.*

Union with Our Lord in his humiliation will lead her to sanctity. "I know that by humiliation alone can Saints be made." [37] Wholly surrendered to Our Lord, she will share in his Divine Love and be able to quench his thirst for love at the same time; and by being an instrument in his hands she will draw other souls to him. It is in this way that her acceptance of humiliation in union with him can have a redemptive value.

Sometimes she describes this redemptive action as gathering the tears which fall from the Holy Face and offering them for souls: "O blessed Face, more lovely than the lilies and the roses of the spring, Thou art not hidden from us. The tears which dim Thine eyes are as precious pearls which we delight to gather, that with them through their infinite value, we may purchase the souls of our brethren." [38]

[36] *Autobiography*, p. 451.
[37] Ibid., p. 335.
[38] Ibid., p. 450.

At other times she likens it to the action of St. Veronica in wiping the Sacred Face of Our Lord. To Céline she writes: "I send you a picture of the Holy Face. The contemplation of this adorable countenance seems to belong in a special way to my little sister, truly the sister of my soul. May she be another Veronica, and wipe away all the blood and tears of Jesus, her only Love! May she give Him souls!"[39] In one of her poems we find the same thought:

> *Vivre d'amour, c'est essuyer ta face,*
> *C'est obtenir des pécheurs le pardon.*[40]

Learn of me, because I am meek, and humble of heart: and you shall find rest to your souls.[41] There is nothing new in this, but it is a hard lesson to learn, and we need to be continually reminded of it. Our Lord has, in our own time, raised up a saint to remind us that unless we are converted and become humble like little children, we cannot enter the kingdom of heaven, for we must be as little children if we are to understand Christ's humility in his Passion. The saint chosen by Almighty God to remind us of this is St. Thérèse of the Child Jesus and of the Holy Face.

[39] Ibid., p. 337.
[40] "All my life love—to wipe thy brow defiled/ With outrage, and for sinners pardon claim."—"Vivre d'amour", *Poems.*
[41] Mt 11:29.

VIII

CONFIDENCE (1)

M Y LITTLE WAY is the way of spiritual childhood, the way of trust and absolute self-surrender." [1] Speaking thus during her last illness to Mother Agnes, her sister, St. Thérèse made it clear that in her eyes, her Little Way was, above all, the way of supernatural confidence. Pilgrims to Lisieux will remember having seen in the very centre of the nave, written boldly in mosaic on the floor of the new basilica, the words *Ayez confiance.* They are there because they epitomize the teaching of the Saint.

St. Thérèse's mission seems to have been to recall the world to childlike confidence in God. Ever since the Fall, man has been estranged from his heavenly Father by fear. *I heard thy voice in paradise; and I was afraid ... and I hid myself.* [2] We are all subject to that fear; it is nothing new. Man has always been conscious of miseries within and without, giving him good cause to fear, and this fear increases the more the effects of sin are realized. May we not say that today men's hearts are *withering away for fear and expectation of what shall come upon the whole world* [3]—a fear experienced at times even in the hearts of the faithful? Many are losing their faith

[1] *Autobiography,* p. 232.
[2] Gen 3:10.
[3] Lk 21:26.

in face of a growing materialism and the apparent success of its persecution of the Church. Confidence weakens and, with it, the whole spiritual life. By stressing the need for confidence in God and giving us a sure ground for this confidence, St. Thérèse enables us to face the troubles of our times in the spirit of Christ. Our confidence must reflect, as did St. Thérèse's, the confidence of Our Lord.

We have already seen that the Way of Spiritual Childhood is based upon the revelation of the Fatherhood of God. We must by faith gaze upon the Father with the eyes of the Son. In the natural order, a child's dependence upon its father is accompanied normally by complete trust and confidence, and the smaller the child, the more unquestioning the confidence; its father could never fail it. It is the same in the supernatural order. Our dependence upon our heavenly Father should normally lead us to an unbounded confidence that since he alone can help us, he surely will; we have only to consider how much he desires to help us to see how far our confidence may go. The more we recognize our need of his help, the more sure we may be that he will come to our aid. Again, in the natural order, it is the helplessness of her child without her that moves a mother's heart. The little child has no need even to look towards its mother, still less to cry out; if there is danger at hand the mother has already seen it, and her arms are around her child before it is aware of its peril. It is the same in the supernatural order. What calls to our heavenly Father with greater insistence than anything else is our helpless dependence upon him.

On a certain occasion during her life in Carmel, St. Thérèse was asked: "Tell us what we must do to be as little children. What do you mean by keeping little?" She replied: "When we keep little we recognize our own nothingness, and expect everything from God just as a little child expects everything from its father. Nothing worries us." [4] In those words she reveals to us the foundation of her confidence. By looking at her heavenly Father's love for her, she learns a secret which is hidden from the wise and prudent and revealed only to little ones, namely, that whereas, in heaven, the love of God goes out to those who are most like himself—the saints, Our Lady, the only-begotten Son, on earth, his love goes out to those who are farthest off—the weak, the outcast, the sinful. In other words, the love revealed to St. Thérèse in the Person of Our Lord was a merciful love, and it is as the "Merciful Love" that she always speaks of it. From her earliest days she had a special knowledge of the Divine Mercy, and one may say that this was the great light of her life and the grace proper to her mission. No one, it would seem, was ever more attracted than she was to this infinite mercy; no one penetrated further into its unfathomable secrets; no one better understood the immensity of the help that human weakness can draw from it. "The mercy of God was the illumining sun of her soul, that which, to her eyes, threw light upon all the mystery of God in His relations with man." [5] That this was so she tells us herself. "All souls cannot be alike. They must differ so that each divine perfection may receive special honour. To me He has manifested His infinite mercy, and in this resplendent mirror I contemplate His other attributes. There each appears radiant with love." [6]

St. Augustine interprets the word *misericordia* as meaning *miseris cor dare*—to give oneself to, or to pour one's heart out over, the weak, the outcast, and the fallen. It is as *merciful* that God reveals himself to us in the Gospels. It is easy to acknowledge this reality in theory, but difficult to live in accordance

[4] *Autobiography*, p. 295.
[5] *Little Way*, by Père Martin, p. 32.
[6] *Autobiography*, p. 147.

with it. It was through constantly meditating on the Gospels and on the mysteries of the faith, with a full consciousness of her weakness and her need, that St. Thérèse was led so intimately into the secret of the Merciful Love of God and, therefore, to such heights of supernatural confidence.

If we open our Gospels with the one thought of this Merciful Love uppermost in our minds, we shall find it on every page. From the outset of his public life we *see* Our Lord ministering to the lame, the deaf, the dumb, the paralysed, the leper, the sick, and the dying. *And when the sun was down, all they that had any sick with divers diseases brought them to him. But he, laying his hands on every one of them, healed them.*[7] But what touched St. Thérèse even more than that was the Merciful Love of God for the moral and spiritual outcast. Two of her favourite parables were those of the Lost Sheep and of the Prodigal Son.[8] In each of these the lesson is the Merciful Love of God for that which is lost. In the first parable the image is that of the Good Shepherd leaving the ninety and nine in the fold and seeking the one lost sheep until he finds it: *Rejoice with me, because I have found my sheep that was lost.* In the second parable it is the image of the father waiting and longing for his lost son: *And when he was yet a great way off, his father saw him, and was moved with compassion* (misericordia motus) *and running to him fell upon his neck and kissed him. . . . It was fit that we should make merry and be glad, for this thy brother was dead and is come to life again; he was lost and is found.*

Still more clearly is this seen in Our Lord's dealings with individual souls. There are several incidents particularly dear to St. Thérèse. It is with the woman of Samaria, belonging to a despised people, heretical in her religion, and none too good in her moral life, that Our Lord holds one of the most

[7] Lk 4:40.
[8] Lk 15.

exquisite dialogues recorded in Scripture, and he finally wins from her an act of faith in his Messiahship.[9] With the woman taken in adultery, though everybody else had branded her, nothing could have been more tender than his treatment, yet nothing more firm than his rebuke: *Hath no man condemned thee? Who said: No man, Lord. And Jesus said: Neither will I condemn thee. Go, and now sin no more.*[10] And with Mary Magdalen, as all around were looking on in disapproval and calling her a sinner, the Christ in his mercy was bending over her and giving her absolution: *Thy sins are forgiven thee.... Go in peace.*[11]

It was meditating on these revelations of the Merciful Love of God that led St. Thérèse to say:

> It is not merely because I have been preserved from mortal sin that I lift up my heart to God in trust and love. I am certain that even if I had on my conscience every imaginable crime, I should lose nothing of my confidence, but would throw myself, heartbroken with sorrow, into the arms of my Saviour. I remember His love for the prodigal son, I have heard His words to Mary Magdalen, to the woman taken in adultery, and to the woman of Samaria. No—there is no one who could frighten me, for I know too well what to believe concerning His mercy and His love.[12]

The Merciful Love of God is the burden of the Gospel story. Our Lord made himself the special friend of publicans and sinners because he had come into the world to seek and to save that which was lost and to call not the righteous but sinners to repentance. *The Lord is gracious and merciful: patient and plenteous in mercy. The Lord is sweet to all; and his tender*

[9] Jn 4.
[10] Jn 8:10–11.
[11] Lk 7:48, 50.
[12] *Autobiography*, p9. 194–95.

mercies are over all his works.[13] That was the supreme message that Holy Scripture held for little Thérèse.

Are we emphasizing God's mercy at the expense of his justice? To think this would indicate a wrong understanding of the relationship between God's mercy and his justice. He is merciful because he is just. It is precisely a wrong view of the Divine Justice that prevents many a soul from realizing fully the Merciful Love of God. True justice takes into account good intentions, the circumstances which lessen the responsibility, no less than those which increase it. God makes allowances for weaknesses and failings, as we rarely do—we are neither just nor merciful enough, because we do not realize our own weaknesses and so do not make allowance for the weaknesses of others; but God sees us as we really are, and before punishing us, in justice he begins by considering our profound misery; his justice excites his mercy. Now St. Thérèse, because she was so conscious of her weakness, saw this truth so clearly that the thought of God's justice, far from terrifying her, only added to her confidence and joy. She tells us this in one of her letters, and as usual she quotes Scripture to support her words.

> I know that He is infinitely just, but the very Justice which terrifies so many souls is the source of all my confidence and joy. Justice is not only stern severity towards the guilty; it takes account of the good intention, and gives to virtue its reward. Indeed I hope as much from the Justice of God as from His Mercy. It is because He is just that *He is compassionate, and merciful, long-suffering, and plenteous in mercy. For He knoweth our frame, He remembereth that we are dust. As a father hath compassion on his children, so hath the Lord compassion on them that fear Him.*[14]

[13] Ps 144:8–9.
[14] *Autobiography*, p. 372.

Again, St. Thérèse says: "In the mirror of His infinite Mercy, all His other attributes appear radiant with love—His Justice perhaps more than all the rest. What joy to think that Our Lord is Just—that He takes into account our weakness and knows so well the frailty of our nature. What then need I fear?" [15] Her childlike reliance on a heavenly Father who loves her because she is but dust led her to experience for herself the mercy of the God of Justice to those who trust themselves to him.

It was, however, her constant meditation on the mysteries of the faith which revealed to St. Thérèse even more directly the depths of the Merciful Love. The Incarnation, the Atonement, the Resurrection, and the Ascension were simply God in his Merciful Love stooping down to succour his weak and helpless children, taking upon himself at Bethlehem their human nature, so that, by bearing their self-inflicted miseries, he might lift them, through his Cross and Resurrection, to their home in heaven for which their Father had made them. The crucifix is the supreme revelation of the intensity of the Merciful Love: it is the embrace of the Father as he takes his erring children once again into his arms. If her heavenly Father would do that for sinners, how much more will he do it for those who try to follow along the path of spiritual childhood? Before this revelation, how could she set any limits to her confidence?

This is St. Paul, through and through. *He that spared not even his own Son, but delivered him up for us all, how hath he not also, with him, given us all things?* [16] Again: *God commendeth his charity towards us: because when as yet we were sinners according to the time, Christ died for us. Much more therefore being now justified by his blood, shall we be saved from wrath through him.* [17] Compelling

[15] Ibid., p. 147.
[16] Rom 8:32
[17] Rom 5:8 9.

as the argument is, it is possible to give a merely intellectual assent to it, and St. Thérèse was sent to teach us that we must really become as little children before we can appreciate this truth in reality.

In the Sacraments of the Church she saw an even more immediate foundation for her confidence. In Baptism, here on earth, at a definite place, at a given moment of time, she found in action the working of God's Merciful Love, for here was planted in her soul, by her Mother the Church, that supernatural gift of grace by which was restored to her the life that had been lost at the Fall, by which she was made a partaker of the Divine Nature, an heir of the kingdom of heaven, in a word, her Father's child. In the Sacrament of Penance she was washed in the Precious Blood of the merciful God who had stooped even to death in order to cleanse her soul. Above all, it was the Holy Eucharist which was the source of her confidence, for here was the continuation on earth of the supreme revelation of the Merciful Love, the sacrifice of Calvary. Here in her Communion she received into her soul the whole redemptive activity of Christ and thus was caught up into the whole plan of the Merciful Love for lifting men from their weakness and miseries and making them partakers of his divinity. Since the Merciful Love of God had contrived to set in the heart of the Church such a wonderful gift as that, she knew that *to them that love God all things work together unto good* [18] and was confident in a love she did not scruple to term foolish.

> O my Saviour! It is Thou whom I love, it is Thou who drawest me so irresistibly to Thee. Thou who, descending into this land of exile, wast willing to suffer and to die in

[18] Rom 8:28.

order to lift up each single soul and plunge it into the very heart of the Blessed Trinity—Love's eternal home! Thou who, ascending into light inaccessible, dost still remain hidden here in this valley of tears under the appearance of the frail white Host to nourish me with Thine own substance. Forgive me, O Jesus, if I tell Thee that Thy love reaches even unto folly, and how canst Thou not wish that before such folly my heart should leap up to Thee? How can my confidence have any bounds? [19]

[19] *Autobiography*, p. 208.

IX

CONFIDENCE (2)

HAVING SEEN THE PLACE which confidence holds in the scheme of the Little Way, we will now examine it more closely. The Little Way is the Way of Spiritual Childhood. The world smiles at it, thinks it weak and sentimental; yet, at the same time, men and women of the world are often unexpectedly converted by it when nothing else has been able to touch them.

The spirit of childhood, as taught by St. Thérèse, attracts us, and yet we hold aloof from it, imagining that our aloofness is a prudent reaction to sentimentality, when often enough it is due to the spirit of the world still strong within us; for the spirit of childhood is attained only through a conversion from which we shrink. Our Lord has told us so himself: *Unless you be converted and become as little children, you shall not enter into the kingdom of heaven.*

To understand the confidence of St. Thérèse we must pray for the spirit of childhood; only then shall we understand what is hid from the wise and prudent and revealed to little ones. "Holiness", she says, "does not consist in one exercise or another, but in a disposition of the heart which renders us humble and little in the hands of God, conscious of our weakness, and confident, even daringly confident, in His fatherly goodness." [1]

[1] *Spirit of St. Thérèse*, comp. by the Carmelites of Lisieux (Burns and Oates), p. 179.

"My way is all love and confidence in God; I do not understand souls who are afraid of so tender a friend."[2] "We can never have too much confidence in the good God, so mighty, so merciful."[3] The *Autobiography* abounds in sayings such as these. At once we recognize the atmosphere of the Gospels, where on nearly every page we find it is faith and confidence in himself that Our Lord seems to value more than anything else.[4] The Gospels show him ever seeking it, endeavouring to arouse it, deeply disappointed when he does not find it, and rewarding it generously whenever it is present. To the centurion Our Lord says: *I have not found so great faith in Israel.*[5] To the woman of Canaan: *O, woman, great is thy faith, be it done to thee as thou wilt.*[6] As they let down the man sick of the palsy through the roof, we are told: *Jesus, seeing their faith, said to the man sick of the palsy: Be of good heart.*[7] When, as in the storm on the lake, he fails to find that faith and confidence in him, he is disappointed: *Why are you fearful? Have you not faith yet?*[8] On the other hand, when he finds it he rejoices and rewards it generously. To the two blind men his message is: *According to your faith, be it done unto you.*[9]

---

[2] *Autobiography*, p. 372.

[3] Ibid., p. 232.

[4] We are in the habit of seeing an intellectual meaning in the word *fides*. It is true that it has such a meaning, sometimes in fact that is its explicit sense, but even then the other meaning of trust in a person, committing oneself to a person, is present and, in a sense, underlies it. In many instances Our Lord is not asking for intellectual assent so much as confidence; the intellectual assent normally follows on this confidence. All the texts mentioned in this chapter are grouped together by F. Zorell, S.J., as implying *fiducia*. Cf. *Lexicon Graecum*, N.T., pp. 1061 and 1064.

[5] Mt 8:10.

[6] Mt 15:28.

[7] Mt 9:2.

[8] Mk 4:40.

[9] Mt 9:29.

The woman with the issue of blood is reassured with the words: *Be of good heart, daughter. Thy faith hath made thee whole.*[10] *Thy faith hath made thee safe,*[11] he says to Mary Magdalen, and so saying, lifts her to sanctity. To blind Bartimaeus his message is the same: *Go thy way, thy faith hath made thee whole.*[12] Most impressive of all, on the night before his death, having foretold to his chosen apostles that they would be hated by the world, that they would be persecuted and suffer sorrow, that they would be stricken and scattered, he ends his last discourse with the words: *But have confidence. I have overcome the world.*[13] Such is the revelation the Gospels give us of Our Lord, yearning over humanity and longing to find in men and women that faith and confidence in him which would enable him to lift them out of their miseries and work wonders for them beyond all human understanding.

Confidence in Our Lord is one of the virtues which we all recognize as essential, yet we do not practise it as we should; we remain, on the contrary, incurably worried and anxious about many things. St. Thérèse, meditating on these texts, saw the primacy of confidence and wrote: "What hurts Jesus, what wounds Him to the heart, is lack of confidence."[14] St. Thérèse's confidence, based upon her complete faith in Our Lord's love for her, was whole-hearted; there was nothing she could not hope for. "Jesus can do all, confidence works miracles."[15] It is just because our faith in his Merciful Love is so weak that we fail in confidence.

Confidence in Christ's individual love and providence had always been very real in the life of St. Thérèse. It was this

[10] Mt 9:22.
[11] Lk 7:50.
[12] Mk 10:52.
[13] Jn 16:33.
[14] *Autobiography,* p. 367.
[15] *Spirit of St. Thérèse,* p. 130.

which supported her through the opposition she had to face before entering Carmel. But she tells us that it was not until the retreat, a year after her profession, that she was encouraged to set forth definitely on that path of supernatural confidence which was to lead her to such heights of sanctity.

> The retreat father understood me completely, and launched me full sail upon the ocean of confidence and love which had so long attracted me, but over which I had scarcely dared venture. He also told me that my faults did not grieve Almighty God, adding: "At this moment I hold His place, and I assure you on His behalf that He is well pleased with your soul." Those words were comforting and filled me with joy, for I had never heard it was possible that faults could not give pain to God. It was, however, the echo of my inmost thoughts. I had long felt that Our Lord is more tender than a mother, and I have sounded the depths of more than one mother's heart. I know by sweet experience how ready a mother is to forgive the involuntary failings of her child.[16]

So she set sail upon the ocean of confidence which had attracted her, but upon which the consciousness of her daily faults had made her hesitate to venture. Here indeed she joins hands with us. It is not our mortal sins so much as our involuntary failings into which, in spite of our genuine desire for holiness, we fall every day; it is these which make us lose confidence, despair of the heights of sanctity, and settle down to a mediocre spirituality.

Conscious that she was her Father's child, and that in spite of her failings she did desire to love him; believing in his infinite mercy and love, she did not allow any morbid consideration of her faults to keep her from him. She did not consider her

[16] *Autobiography*, p. 138.

faults in their negative aspect and so remain discouraged. She passed swiftly to the positive aspect. She regarded those faults as reminders of her weakness and of her essential need for Our Lord's constant support; they caused her to turn more completely to him that he might alone be her sanctification. She was liberated from all diffidence, and her confidence, now unhindered, carried her swiftly towards perfection.

In one of her letters she says:

> Since it has been given to me to understand the love of the Heart of Jesus, I confess that all fear has been driven from mine. The remembrance of my faults humbles me and helps me never to rely upon my own strength which is mere weakness. Still more does that remembrance speak to me of mercy and love. When with childlike confidence we cast our faults into Love's all-devouring furnace, how can they fail to be utterly consumed? [17]

Now perhaps we understand more easily one of the expressions of her intimate audacity with Our Blessed Lord. "I confide in Jesus," she says, "I relate to Him in detail my infidelities, thinking in my daring abandonment to acquire in this way more power over His Heart and to win more fully the love of Him who is not come to call the just but sinners to repentance." [18]

The devil would sap her confidence by making her conscious of her faults and failings and so hinder her progress to perfection. She completely turns the tables on him. Deliberately she directs her attention to her failings, gathers them together, leaves them at Jesus' feet as a demonstration of her helplessness, and pursues her way to sanctity, her confidence only increased by this fresh realization of her weakness, which she herself calls "a great grace".

[17] *Spirit of St. Thérèse*, p. 129.
[18] Ibid.

It is at prayer more than at any other time that the consciousness of our weakness and our apparent failure saps our
confidence. If the devil can play on this and destroy our personal prayer, he has gone far to stopping our spiritual progress.
Sometimes we are discouraged by the weakness of our flesh.
We set apart a time for prayer, and we at once become drowsy
and fall asleep, or else our mind is filled with distractions over
which we seem to have no control. At other times spiritual
dryness impairs our confidence; we are tempted to ascribe it
to our want of fervour and fidelity, and so we grow disheartened. St. Thérèse shared this experience. Weariness at prayer
was a very real difficulty to her, but she knew how to meet
it. "I suppose I ought to be distressed that I fall asleep at meditation and during my thanksgiving after Holy Communion,
but I reflect that little children, asleep or awake, are equally
dear to their parents." [19]

For St. Thérèse the solution to the difficulty lay in the two
words "Our Father". Our Lord had laid those words upon her
lips as the model of all prayer, and she took them literally. How
then could her confidence have any bounds? Provided she was
faithful to her Little Way of Spiritual Childhood, provided,
that is to say, she prayed with the simplicity of a child, what
could it matter to her heavenly Father if she fell asleep in efforts
to prove her love? As for distractions she says: "I accept them
all, even the wildest fancies that cross my mind, for the love
of God." [20]

It was the same with her dryness in prayer. From the
moment of her entry into Carmel, the way chosen for St.
Thérèse by her heavenly Father, so far from being a way of
sweetness, was instead a way of continual aridity. "From the
very outset," she tells us, "my soul had for its daily nourish-

[19] *Autobiography*, p. 134
[20] Ibid., p. 316.

ment nothing but bitter dryness." [21] One of the occasions on which she mentions it in the *Autobiography* is the very last occasion on which we should have expected it. It is the retreat before her clothing. Of this she says: "Dryness and drowsiness—such is the state of my soul in its intercourse with Jesus." [22]

In the midst of her dryness and desolation she is happy and glad, when we should have been depressed and discouraged. What is the reason for this difference? It is this: St. Thérèse really believed in the Fatherhood of God; we believe in it only feebly. We have not become sufficiently childlike. St. Thérèse was convinced that the Father who had made her to love him, and upon whom she so utterly depended, could not fail to answer the prayers of a child who loved him, provided they were humble and sincere. No matter what dryness she experienced she relied on the words of Our Lord: *And which of you, if he ask his father bread, will he give him a stone? Or a fish, will he for a fish give him a serpent? Or if he shall ask an egg, will he reach him a scorpion? If you then, being evil, know how to give good gifts to your children, how much more will your Father from heaven give the good Spirit to them that ask him?* [23]

Her confidence developed as she considered the doctrine of the Fatherhood of God. If a human father's heart is loving and generous, how much more the heart of our Father in heaven? St. Thérèse's confidence did not depend on whether or not she felt consolation, or on whether or not her prayers seemed to be answered; it was based upon the words of Our Blessed Lord.

St. Thérèse has been sent to reawaken in us this confidence which we all need so badly. We hesitate and fear in the matter

[21] Ibid., p. 122.
[22] Ibid., p. 134.
[23] Lk 11:11–13.

of our prayers, because we are too much influenced by our feelings, and by our own ideas as to how and when and where our prayers should be answered: and when we have no consolation, or our ideas are not realized, we become distressed. To share the confidence of St. Thérèse we must place our trust where she placed hers, in the promises of Jesus Christ. Such confidence is an essential part of the Little Way of Spiritual Childhood, and it is granted to "little ones". For our encouragement let us remember that St. Thérèse did not arrive at this confidence through merely human efforts. She was constantly aided by the Holy Trinity dwelling in her soul, and we must never forget that the least degree of grace gives us this source of strength within us. Confidence is a gift of the Holy Spirit, refused to none and granted in proportion to our faith. *For you have not received the spirit of bondage again in fear, but you have received the spirit of adoption of sons whereby we cry Abba (Father).*[24]

St. Thérèse's aspirations, however lofty and exalted, were not the result of extraordinary graces but of a confidence exercised in the knowledge of her weakness and infirmities which, so far from causing her to despair, threw her more completely upon Our Lord and opened her soul to the active workings of his Merciful Love within her. She tells us that when she was a little girl at school she had the daring confidence that she would one day be a saint. She had a great devotion to Joan of Arc and longed to imitate her.

> Then, [she tells us] as I reflected that I was born for great things, and sought the means to attain them, it was made known to me interiorly that my personal glory would never reveal itself before the eyes of men, but would consist in becoming a Saint. This aspiration may very well appear

[24] Rom 8:15.

rash, seeing how imperfect I was, and am even now after so many years of religious life; yet I still feel the same daring confidence that one day I shall become a great Saint. I am not trusting in my own merits, for I have none: but I trust in Him who is Virtue and Holiness itself. It is He alone who, pleased with my poor efforts, will raise me to Himself, and by clothing me with His merits make me a Saint. [25]

As the years passed by, this desire to be a great saint deepened till at last it found expression in a resolve to offer herself as a victim to the Merciful Love of God. At this point we may draw back, but we should be wrong to do so. We shall see, on the contrary, how she takes us by the hand and shows us that the weakness which makes us hesitate and shrink is the very means which brought her to her goal.

She tells us how, when thinking of those who offer themselves as victims to the justice of God to turn aside punishment from sinners and take it upon themselves, she was not attracted by the thought. Instead, however, she found herself overwhelmingly drawn to offer herself as a victim to the Merciful Love of God: that is to say, to surrender herself so completely to the workings of his Merciful Love in her soul that, all self being eliminated, the tenderness imprisoned in the Sacred Heart might flood her soul and, through her, flow out to the souls of others. So, on Trinity Sunday, 1895, she made the Act of Oblation set out in full earlier in this book. We repeat here the passages immediately to our purpose:

> I wish to be holy, but knowing how helpless I am, I beseech Thee, my God, to be Thyself my holiness.... During the days of His life on earth, Thy divine Son, my sweet Spouse, spoke these words: *If you ask the Father anything in My name,*

---

[25] *Autobiography*, p. 70.

He will give it you. Therefore I am certain Thou wilt grant my prayer. O my God, I know that the more Thou wishest to bestow, the more Thou dost make us desire. In my heart I feel boundless desires, and I confidently beseech Thee to take possession of my soul.... In order that my life may be one act of perfect love, I offer myself as a holocaust to Thy Merciful Love, imploring Thee to consume me unceasingly and to allow the floods of infinite tenderness gathered up in Thee to overflow into my soul, so that I may become a martyr to Thy love, O my God.[26]

In those sentences we see St. Thérèse's desire for holiness; side by side with it we see her sense of helplessness which, however, is not allowed to frustrate her desire, but which serves only to throw her back with unquestioning confidence on the promises of Our Lord.

The last pages of the *Autobiography*, which on first reading seem to be only a series of lofty aspirations entirely unrelated to us, now take on a different aspect. We see, inseparably interwoven with these aspirations, a sense of her failings, weakness, and helplessness, which she makes the starting point of her confidence in and abandonment to the love of Our Lord. Here at least she joins hands with us.

I am but a weak and helpless child, but my very weakness makes me dare to offer myself, O Jesus, as victim to Thy love.... How can a soul so imperfect as mine aspire to the plenitude of Love? What is the key to this mystery? O my only Friend! Why dost Thou not reserve these infinite longings for lofty souls, for the eagles that soar in the heights? Alas! I am only a little unfledged bird. Yet the eagle's spirit is mine and notwithstanding my littleness I dare to gaze upon the Divine Sun of Love, I burn to dart

[26] Ibid., p. 447.

upwards into its fires. Fain would I fly as the eagle does,
but I can only flutter my wings—it is beyond my feeble
strength to soar. What then is to become of me? Must I
die of sorrow because of my helplessness? No! I will not
even grieve. With daring confidence, and reckless of self,
I will remain there till death, my gaze fixed upon the Divine
Sun. Nothing shall affright me, neither wind nor rain; and
should impenetrable clouds conceal from my eyes the Orb
of Love, should it seem to me that beyond this life there is
darkness only, that would be the hour of perfect joy, the
hour in which to push my confidence to its farthest bounds
for, knowing that beyond the dark clouds my Sun is still
shining, I should never dare to change my place.

O my God, thus far do I understand Thy Love for me,
but Thou knowest how often I lose sight of what is my only
care, and straying from Thy side allow my wings to be
bedraggled in the muddy pools of this world. *Then I cry like
a young swallow* and my cry tells Thee all, and Thou dost
remember, O Infinite Mercy, *that Thou didst not come to call
the just but sinners.*[27]

After she has thus made common ground with us through
our infirmities and weakness, we find her carrying us along
with her before we realize what is happening.

O Jesus! Would that I could tell all little souls of Thy inef-
fable condescension! If by any possibility Thou couldst find
one weaker than mine, one which should abandon itself in
perfect trust to Thy Infinite Mercy, I feel that Thou wouldst
take delight in loading that soul with still greater favours.
But whence these desires, O my Spouse, to make known
the secrets of Thy Love? Is it not Thou alone who hast
taught them to me and canst Thou not likewise reveal them
to others? I know Thou canst and I beseech Thee to do

[27] Ibid., pp.204, 206–7.

so—I beseech Thee to cast Thy glance upon a vast number of little souls: I entreat Thee to choose in this world a legion of little victims worthy of Thy love.[28]

These words are not just the outpourings of a great saint, with no meaning for us. They are, on the contrary, a direct invitation to every one of us, each in his own degree to follow her to the heights of sanctity. She shows us that we are to do this, through a childlike confidence which is not discouraged by weaknesses and failings, but which, trusting in Our Lord's promises, sees those very weaknesses as a sure means of placing us more securely in his arms.

[28] Ibid., p. 208.

X

SELF-SURRENDER

C LOSELY ALLIED WITH the love, humility, and confidence of the Little Way of Spiritual Childhood is its spirit of self-surrender. For St. Thérèse, as we have seen, this means the surrender of a small child throwing itself into its father's arms in times of joy as well as of trial, and remaining peacefully there, certain that it is safe. "Jesus was pleased to show me the only path which leads to the divine furnace of Love; this path is the abandonment of the little child who sleeps without fear in its Father's arms."[1] To rest in the arms of God as a child in its father's arms demands the continual surrender of our will to the will of God, which is the essence of the spiritual life.

> When the way of perfection was opened before me [wrote St. Thérèse], I realized that to become a Saint I must suffer much.... I cried out: "My God, I choose everything, I will not be a Saint by halves, I am not afraid of suffering for Thee. One thing only do I fear, and that is to follow my own will. Accept then the offering I make of it, for I choose all that Thou willest."[2]

So to surrender ourselves to God that we constantly will what he wills is perfection. St. Thérèse teaches us to look upon the

[1] *Autobiography*, p. 197.
[2] Ibid., p. 40.

will of God as best and most lovable, especially when, to us, it seems the opposite. In the self-surrender she teaches, austerity, as such, is of secondary importance; the primary consideration is that if God wants it, then we want it too. The austerity indeed is there, but it is all enveloped in the Father's love.

> *Rappelle-toi que ta volonté sainte*
> *Est mon repos, mon unique bonheur;*
> *Je m'abandonne et je m'endors sans crainte*
> *Entre tes bras, O mon divin Sauveur.*[3]

That this is so is clearly shown to us in the surrender of Our Lord to the Father's will during his Passion and Crucifixion. As his Passion approaches, he says explicitly to his disciples: *Therefore doth the Father love me: because I lay down my life.*[4] The Cross indeed is there, the scourging, the crown of thorns, the nails, and the soldier's spear, but they all lie within the Father's love, and thus Our Lord's complete surrender to them becomes the supreme expression of the love of the Only-begotten for his Father. *That the world may know that I love the Father: and as the Father hath given me commandment, so do I. Arise, let us go hence.*[5] And he arose and went straight to his Passion.

Jesus knowing that his hour was come, that he should pass out of this world, to the Father . . . knowing that the Father had given him all things into his hands and that he came from God and goeth to God. . . .[6] The horror of the Passion and the agony of Calvary are simply the going forth of the beloved Son to the Father,

---

[3] "Remember, Lord, that Thy most holy will/ Alone is joy to me, alone is rest./ Fearlessly trusting, see, I sleep so still,/ Saviour divine, close folded to Thy breast."—"Jesus, rappelle-toi", *Poems*. Translated by D. A. P.

[4] Jn 10:17.

[5] Jn 14:31.

[6] Jn 13:1, 3.

the beloved Son into whose hands the Father has given all
things. St. Peter, like so many of us, could not see it. He draws
his sword in a vain attempt to put a stop to what seems to him
so wrong. Our Lord replies: *The chalice which my Father hath
given me, shall I not drink it?*[7] *Thinkest thou that I cannot ask my
Father, and he will give me presently twelve legions of angels? How
then shall the scriptures be fulfilled, that so it must be done?*[8] finally,
at the moment of his death, when the tragedy seemed com-
plete and evil seemed so clearly to have triumphed, Our Lord,
with perfect confidence, prays: *Father, into thy hands I commend
my spirit.*[9]

What does all this tell us if it be not that the Father's arms
were about him, that the beginning and end of it all was love?

Before developing this theme further, it may be well to
answer an objection sometimes raised to this image of a child
in its father's arms. The analogy is not to be understood in any
quietistic sense. What the little child does by instinct in the
natural sphere, the soul must do by grace in the supernatural.
The sleep of the little child is a parable of that peace which
comes from a will completely surrendered to God's will, from
moment to moment. This demands an activity comparable
with that of a drowning man who, suppressing his natural
instinct to trust to his own efforts and realizing that his only
hope is in the man who swims to his rescue, surrenders himself completely—an act demanding courage and perfect self-
control.

At times this surrender may appear to be merely passive.
"I offer myself to Thee, O my Beloved, that Thou mayest
perfectly accomplish in me Thy Holy Will."[10] But it is not

[7] Jn 18:11.
[8] Mt 26:53–54.
[9] Lk 23:46.
[10] *Autobiography*, p. 30.

so. A few years later, writing to her sister, St. Thérèse says: "My desire is to do always the will of Jesus. Let us leave Him free to take and give whatever He wills. Perfection consists in doing His will, surrendering ourselves wholly to Him." [11] "The more content a soul is to accomplish His will the more perfect it is." [12]

She would do his will with wholehearted devotion as well as accept all that comes from his hand, remembering however that, even in doing her share, she was entirely dependent on his constant help.

Surrender in its perfection, it is true, can be achieved only by those who reach the summit of sanctity, but it is most important for us to understand that, in St. Thérèse's eyes, surrender is a characteristic of the Little Way from the beginning. It is, as she says, the only path which leads to the divine furnace of Love. Surrender in varying degrees as we progress is a marked characteristic in all those who follow the Little Way.

It was so in the life of St. Thérèse herself long before she entered Carmel. When quite a little girl she used to think of herself as the Holy Child's ball, which he could play with as he liked. That this idea was no mere childish conceit we know from the way in which she turned to it for her encouragement in a moment of severe trial. After the failure of her appeal to the Holy Father during the pilgrimage to Rome, when all her efforts to enter Carmel seemed fruitless, she writes:

> My journey had failed in its purpose. . . . For some time past I had offered myself to the Child Jesus to be His little ball. I told Him to treat me just as it might please Him. In a word I desired to amuse the Holy Child, to let Him play with

[11] Letter to Céline, July 6, 1893.
[12] *Autobiography*, p. 136.

me just as He felt inclined. My prayer had been heard. You can imagine, dear Mother, the desolation of that little ball as it lay abandoned on the ground! Yet it continued to hope against hope.[13]

From Rome she wrote to her sister Pauline, who had only recently entered Carmel: "Great indeed is my trial, but I am the little ball of Jesus; if He wishes to break His plaything to pieces he is quite free to do so. Yes, I want only what He wills."[14] And this at the age of fourteen! Because of this surrender she tells us she never became discouraged: "All the time deep down in my heart reigned a wonderful peace because I knew that I was seeking only God's will."[15]

St. Thérèse's life abounded in trials. From the moment of her entry into Carmel she was misunderstood by those around her; all through her convent life she suffered acutely, both physically and spiritually; and the last three years were spent in unrelieved spiritual desolation. In all those trials she never wavered in her self-surrender. "At the moment of my greatest trials, when it was my turn to intone the psalms in choir, if you only knew with what surrender I would say out loud the verse: *In Thee, O Lord, have I hoped.*"[16] In those words, *In Thee, O Lord, have I hoped*, we have perhaps the main secret of St. Thérèse's self-surrender, namely, that she put her whole trust in Our Lord himself, not in any particular manifestation of his will. This is where we often fail. We lose heart, and our surrender is seen to be imperfect. We trust in some particular good which we imagine to be God's will; and when that fails, we think that all is lost. Yet it is often when all seems lost

---

[13] Ibid., p. 115.

[14] *Spirit of St. Thérèse,* comp. by the Carmelites of Lisieux (Burns and Oates), p. 136.

[15] *Autobiography,* p. 102.

[16] *Spirit of St. Thérèse,* p. 143.

that Our Lord's will is most surely being fulfilled. To St. Thérèse the where or how of God's will did not matter. She knew it would be done because she knew him in whom she trusted; the one thing she sought was to correspond faithfully with every grace she was given and to go forward.

She seems to have learned this specially from the Gospel story of the storm on the lake. Our Lord bids his disciples enter a boat and cross the lake. Yet they sail into the teeth of a storm, while he himself falls asleep on a pillow in the hinder part of the ship. The wind rises and the waves beat over the ship. Still the Master sleeps, until the disciples wake him with the cry: *Master, doth it not concern thee that we perish?* A very natural cry, and a perfectly good prayer. The psalms are full of such prayers for rescue in the hour of peril. Our Lord stills the wind and the waves, then turns to his disciples, not to say: "I am so glad that you woke me in time", but *Why are you fearful? Have you not faith yet?* [17] In Our Lord's eyes the perfect thing would have been to carry on in spite of the storm, knowing that with him in the ship all would be well, even though he was asleep.

By thinking of the implications of this incident, St. Thérèse learned how to face the storms in her spiritual life. Writing of the retreat before her profession, she says:

> I went through it in a state of utter spiritual desolation—as if abandoned by God. Jesus slept in my boat, as was His wont. But how rarely will souls allow Him to sleep in peace! Wearied with making continual advances, our good Master readily avails Himself of the repose I offer Him, and will in all probability sleep on till my great and everlasting retreat. This, however, rather rejoices than grieves me.[18]

In this whole-hearted surrender she just carries on without fuss or fret. This image of her soul as a barque in which

[17] Mk 4:38, 40.
[18] *Autobiography*, p. 134.

Our Lord was resting and asleep was a favourite one with the Saint, and she often referred to it, saying: "Ah well, I shall take good care never to awaken Him."

> *Vivre d'amour lorsque Jésus sommeille,*
> *C'est le repos sur les flots orageux.*
> *Oh! ne crains pas, Seigneur, que je t'éveille,*
> *J'attends en paix le rivage des cieux.*[19]

In a letter to her sister Céline, St. Thérèse uses the same image with a slightly different application. "In order to guide his barque the one thing proper for a little child is to abandon himself, to let his sail be filled at the mercy of the wind."[20] Nothing could be more prudent, for the wind she refers to is the breath of God moving over the waters. *The Spirit breatheth where he will,*[21] and the Spirit of God is love. In allowing itself to be borne along by the wind it is to Love itself, to a Love which is infinite in wisdom and goodness as well as in power, that the childlike soul entrusts itself.

Another image by which the Saint tries to express the beauty of surrender is that of the scattered rose. Many beautiful roses, she says in one of her poems, adorn God's altar, and those who see them look at their beauty with admiration; but for herself she desires something very different. She wishes to be a rose whose petals are scattered far and wide, with no beauty except that of the pattern formed by the petals as they lie haphazard, blown hither and thither at the mercy of the wind. She wants to place her life unreservedly

---

[19] "All my life love! No sign though Jesus make,/ He is but sleeping on the storm-tossed sea;/ Jesus, sleep on; for me thou shalt not wake;/ Till the clouds part, I will wait patiently."—"Vivre d'amour", *Poems*. Translated by Msgr. R. A. Knox.

[20] *Spirit of St. Thérèse*, p. 138.

[21] Jn 3:8.

at the mercy of the Spirit of Love, that he may do with it whatever he will.

> *La rose en son eclat peut embellir ta fête,*
> *Aimable Enfant!*
> *Mais la rose effeuillée, on l'oublie, on la jette*
> *Au gré du vent.*
>
> *La rose, en s'effeuillant, sans recherche se donne*
> *Pour n'être plus,*
> *Comme elle, avec bonheur, à toi je m'abandonne,*
> *Petit Jésus!* [22]

Thus, by varying images of the little barque, the scattered rose, and the child resting in its father's arms, does St. Thérèse seek to express the beauty of childlike surrender to the love of God. But it is the last that appears most frequently in her writings. To it she returns again and again as expressing most fully the truth she is endeavouring to teach.

It is such folly to pass time fretting, instead of resting quietly on the Heart of Jesus. Neither ought the little child to be afraid in the dark, nor complain at not seeing the Beloved who carries her in His arms. She has only to shut her eyes—that is the one sacrifice God asks of her. If she does this, the dark will lose its terrors, because she will not see it, and before long, peace, if not joy, will return once more. [23]

---

[22] "Dear Lord, the flowers that blossom yet/ Thy feast-day with their perfume fill;/ The rose that's fallen, men forget,/ And winds may scatter where they will./ The rose that's fallen questions not,/ Content, as for Thy sake, to die,/ Abandonment its welcome lot—/ Dear Infant Christ, that rose be I!"—translated by Msgr. R. A. Knox.

[23] *Autobiography*, p. 296.

The spirit of surrender permeated her prayer from the very first. "I have never", she writes, "sought to ask favours of the good God. If for instance, I had said on the day of my First Communion: 'My God, grant me the favour of dying young', I should regret it very greatly today, because I should not be sure of having done His will alone." [24] Referring to the day of her profession, rather more than a year after her entry into Carmel, she tells us: "I was told to beg for the recovery of our darling father; but I was unable to make any other prayer than this: 'O my God, I beseech Thee that it may be Thy will for my father to recover.'" [25] In her early days she seems to have had a desire to die young, but later she says: "From my earliest years I believed that the Little Flower would be gathered in her springtime, but now the spirit of self-surrender is my sole guide—I have no other compass. I am no longer able to ask eagerly for anything save the perfect accomplishment of God's designs on my soul." [26]

St. Thérèse had a great devotion to the saints, and she rested in the support of their prayers, especially during her last illness. This was not because she was particularly conscious of their assistance; indeed it was just the opposite. But the feeling she had that they had abandoned her did not discourage her; it only made her love them all the more. "I often", she says, "pray to the Saints without being heard.... But the more deaf they appear to my voice, the more I love them." [27]

So far from being stern and grim, her self-surrender was full of gaiety. Mother Agnes told her one morning that she was praying that she might suffer less, and yet she seemed to

[24] *Spirit of St. Thérèse*, p. 141.
[25] Ibid., p. 143.
[26] Ibid.
[27] *Autobiography*, p. 146.

suffer more. St. Thérèse replied: "You see I am asking God not to hear the prayers that would place an obstacle to the accomplishment of His designs upon me." [28]

One of the results of her spirit of surrender was a refusal to worry about the future; though we must distinguish here: it is one thing to take ordinary and prudent precautions for the morrow, it is quite another thing to worry about it. It was this latter that St. Thérèse refused to do. "We who run in the way of Love ought not to think of sorrows that the future may bring, for then there is a lack of confidence, and that is how we confuse ourselves with imagination." [29]

This refusal to worry about the future is one of the most important and precious fruits of the Spirit of Childhood. There is nothing in our ordinary everyday life which so exhausts our energy—physical, mental, and spiritual—as anxiety about the future. We worry ourselves over fears that are never realized, or, if the difficulties which we foresee do come to pass, they do so in a manner so different from what we expected that all our worry beforehand has been of no avail. Many men have broken down through anxiety over imaginary troubles. It is vital to our spiritual life that we be liberated from such fears.

Self-surrender lifts us above all that:

It is a great mistake to worry as to what trouble there may be in store for us: it is like meddling with God's work. We who run in the way of love must never allow ourselves to be disturbed by anything. If I did not simply suffer from one moment to another, it would be impossible for me to be patient: but I look only at the present, I forget the past and I take good care not to forestall the future. When we

---

[28] *Novissima verba*, comp. by the Carmelites of Lisieux (Burns and Oates), p. 129.
[29] Ibid., p. 82.

yield to discouragement or despair it is usually because we give too much thought to the past and to the future.[30]

This surrender to the Father's loving will from day to day, this refusal to be anxious about the future, was one of the lessons which Our Lord was most concerned to teach when he was on earth. *Be not therefore solicitous for tomorrow: for the morrow will be solicitous for itself. Sufficient for the day is the evil thereof.*[31] We all know the Christian philosophy of living just for today; that thereby we lessen the power of our temptations, while pain is easier to bear if we have to suffer only for today. The more important thing however is to think of today as the only day which we have in which to *love* God. Then what quality will we put into our love!

> *Ma vie est un instant, une heure passagère,*
> *Ma vie est un moment, qui m'échappe et qui fuit.*
> *Je n'ai pour aimer Dieu sur cette pauvre terre*
> *Que ce jour qui s'enfuit!*[32]

If, in the spirit of complete abandonment, we love God today as if we had no other day in which to love him, then automatically all our pain becomes easier to bear, all our temptations lose their strength. It is love which is the key to all.

St. Thérèse was so wholly surrendered to God's will that her life became a continuous act of love. At no time was this more true than during the great trials which marked the end of her life—acute physical suffering combined with terrible temptations against the faith. She was in an advanced stage of

---

[30] *Autobiography*, p. 222.

[31] Mt 6:34.

[32] "An instant is my life, a passing hour, no more,/ A moment swift, whose flight no mortal hand can stay./ To love my God on earth, to love Him and adore,/ I have but this brief day."—"Mon chant d'aujourd'hui", *Poems*. Translated by D. A. P.

consumption, and added to this was a state of profound spiritual desolation. In her early days the thought of death had been welcome to her, for she had seen death as the gateway to heaven; now, when her sufferings closed in upon her, that seemed no more than a dream. "Once I was able to see clearly afar off the lighthouse which showed me the harbour of heaven, but now I see nothing. God wills me so to surrender myself as to be altogether like a little child who is not disturbed by whatever is done to him." [33]

Wasted with fever, in continual pain, she became quite helpless. "O my Mother, what would become of me if God did not give me His strength? I have only my hands free. Never would I have believed it possible to suffer so much. And even yet I do not believe I am at the end of my suffering: but He will never abandon me." [34] So severe were her sufferings that she was asked whether she did not long for death. She replied:

> I desire neither life nor death. Were Our Lord to offer me my choice, I would not choose. I only will what He wills, and I am pleased with whatever He does. I have no fear of the last struggle or of any pain, however great, which my illness may bring. God has always been my help. He has led me by the hand ever since I was a child, and I count on Him now. Even though suffering should reach its furthest limits, I am certain He will never forsake me. [35]

Along with this physical suffering went great spiritual desolation. St. Thérèse says that she was enveloped in "a darkness which found its way into my very soul". [36] "For my soul it was night, always the darkest night." [37] "Pray for me," she

---

[33] *Novissima verba*, p. 29.
[34] Ibid., p. 146.
[35] *Autobiography*, p. 223.
[36] Ibid., p. 156.
[37] Ibid., p. 199.

said to her sisters, "for often when I cry to Heaven for help it is then that I feel most abandoned." "How do you manage", they asked her, "not to give way to discouragement when you are forsaken in this way?"

> I turn [she replied] to God and to all the Saints and I thank them notwithstanding; I believe they want to see how far I shall trust them. But the words of Job have not entered my heart in vain: even if God should kill me, I would still trust Him. I admit that it has taken a long time to arrive at this degree of self-surrender, but I have reached it now and it is Our Lord Himself who has brought me there.[38]

Because she knew that this suffering was her Father's loving providence for her, St. Thérèse embraced it and in it found her joy. After a painful day, her sister said to her: "You have suffered much today." St. Thérèse replied: "Yes, but I love it. I love whatsoever God gives me."[39] In spite of this, she knew the value of the virtue of prudence; feeling herself ever little and weak even in the arms of her heavenly Father, she never desired or asked for greater sufferings than those which Almighty God destined for her.

> At each moment [she says], He sends me what I am able to bear—nothing more—and if He increases the pain, my strength is also increased. But I could never ask for greater sufferings. I am too little a soul. They would then be my own choice; I should have to bear them all without Him, and I have never been able to do anything when left to myself.[40]

Again during her last illness she said: "I have found joy and happiness on earth, but solely in suffering, because I have

[38] Ibid., p. 222.
[39] *Novissima verba*, p. 134.
[40] *Autobiography*, p. 233.

suffered much down here. You must make this known to souls."[41]

Acute suffering of soul and body, and yet all enveloped in love and joy. How can those two be reconciled? So impossible does it seem to us that we are almost inclined to suspect that the sufferings were exaggerated, or that St. Thérèse was deluded as to her joy.

We are in the presence of a great mystery. The Saint seems to have foreseen that difficulty and to have had a premonition that she was in some way suffering as an example for the encouragement of other souls in the future. "It must be made known", she says, "that these transports and joys are only in the depths of my soul. It would not greatly encourage souls if they believed I had not suffered much."[42] She then lifts the veil a little on that great mystery. "To suffer peacefully is not always to find consolation in the suffering, for peace is not always accompanied by joy, not at least by sensible joy. To suffer with peace it suffices that we truly will all that God wills."[43] In another passage St. Thérèse takes us a little further.

Our Lord's will fills my heart to the brim, and if anything else be added it cannot penetrate to any depth, but like oil on the surface of limpid waters, glides easily across. If my heart were not already brimming over, if it needed to be filled by the feelings of joy and sadness that follow each other so rapidly, then indeed it would be flooded by bitter sorrow, but these quick-succeeding changes scarcely ruffle the surface of my soul, and in its depths there reigns a peace that nothing can disturb.[44]

---

[41] *Novissima verba*, p. 96.
[42] Ibid., p. 134.
[43] *Autobiography*, p. 336.
[44] Ibid., p. 222.

Here she leads us, as always, to Holy Scripture, to the mystery of Gethsemane. On the sixth of July, a short three months before her death, she said: "I have just read a beautiful passage in the *Imitation of Christ*: 'Our Lord in the Garden of Olives enjoyed all the delights of the Blessed Trinity, and nevertheless His agony was not less cruel.' That is a mystery, but I assure you that I understand something of it, through that which I have experienced myself." [45]

In the words of St. Thérèse it is a mystery, and as a mystery we must leave it. But she does help us to understand

---

[45] *Novissima verba*, p. 40. Tanquerey has an interesting passage in which he refers to these words of St. Thérèse: "But, it may be objected, the soul of Jesus enjoyed the Beatific Vision and consequently could not suffer like a human soul. It is, of course, quite true to say that, even during the Passion, Jesus enjoyed the Beatific Vision. But, as St. Thomas rightly observes, this vision which lit the summit of His higher faculties, the pinnacle of intelligence and will, did not shine on the less elevated regions which Our Lord quite freely and deliberately abandoned to suffering. Thus the blessed soul of our Saviour might be compared to a mountain whose summit was brilliantly lit by the sun, while the tempest raged on the lower slopes. In the higher regions of His soul there was perfect happiness, yet at the same time there remained intense sufferings, not confined merely to the feelings but present even in the less elevated regions of the higher faculties.

"The distinction which mystics made between the summit of the soul, capable of contemplation, and the understanding which suffers real tortures, especially during the night of the senses and of the mind, throws great light on this mysterious problem, and shows how the same souls can at one and the same moment be quite happy in the fulfilment of the divine will and yet suffer a veritable purgatory not merely in their feelings but even in the intelligence. These souls would not lessen their sufferings for anything in the world. With St. Teresa of Avila they continually aspire 'to suffer or to die, but rather to suffer'. Or they say perhaps with St. John of the Cross: 'Let us suffer and be despised.' Nearer to our own times St. Thérèse of Lisieux, two months before her death, said: 'I have read a beautiful passage in the *Imitation*: "Our Lord, in the Garden of Olives, enjoyed all the delights of the Blessed Trinity yet His agony was none the less cruel." It is a mystery, but I can assure you that I understand something of it through that which I have experienced myself'" (Tanquerey, *La Divinisation de la souffrance*, pp. 3–4).

something of it. A soul which is entirely surrendered to the will of God, and therefore completely filled with his love, can be carried through physical suffering and the dark night of faith, in such a way that although the storm rages and the night is dark, the soul is happy and at peace, with *the peace...which surpasseth all understanding.*[46]

> *Entre ses bras divins je ne crains pas l'orage.*
> *Le total abandon, voilà ma seule loi!*
> *Sommeiller sur son cœur tout près de son visage.*
> *Voilà mon ciel à moi.*[47]

We see now something of what Thérèse means by self-surrender. Those who are among that "vast number of little souls" chosen by God through the intercession of St. Thérèse are all, in varying degrees, called to follow along that path of childlike surrender. One thing is necessary—that we be converted and become as little children, for only little children can be carried in the Father's arms and so enter the kingdom of heaven.

---

[46] Phil 4:7.

[47] "One law alone I know—within my Lord's embrace/ In perfect trust to lie. No storm there shall I fear./ Slumbering on His breast, near to His Holy Face,/ That is my heaven here."—"Mon ciel à moi", *Poems*. Translated by D. A. P.

XI

THE VALUE OF LITTLE THINGS

THOSE WHO FOLLOW the Way of Spiritual Childhood look upon God, as, above all else, their Father, and their child-like surrender to him runs through everything and gives to the love, humility, and confidence of the Little Way its unique note of spontaneous gaiety.

They know that love is repaid by love alone and long to respond to their Father's love for them by lives which are one continuous act of humble love. They try to surrender them-selves so completely to God's love that it may take entire pos-session of them, so that they become as St. Thérèse prayed they might—victims of the Merciful Love of God.

Now comes the question, how exactly is that to be done? It sounds very attractive in theory, and in theory we know it is right. Nothing less than that is the vocation to which we are called, but the very ideal it sets before us seems to imply something out of the ordinary, and life, for most of us, is ordi-nary—very ordinary.

How does the Little Way, with its invitation to become a victim of the Merciful Love of God, fit into our ordinary everyday lives? The answer is simple. Our Lord told his apos-tles that they must be converted and become as little chil-dren if they were to enter the kingdom of heaven. In the natural order how do little children show their love?

Through little things. A little child, just because it is little, is utterly unable to show its love in any other way. At some time or other we have all had evidence of that, if only we have had eyes to see it. The most superficial observation of human life shows us how very little children will continually offer little things to their mother—a toy, a picture, a flower—as evidence of their love. To show their love they relate everything to their mother, and the means they make use of are the insignificant details of their little world, the things that lie immediately to hand. We notice too that the mother, although she has no need of the toy, the picture, or the flower, loves the child to make these offerings, because she wants the love that lies behind them. In themselves they are nothing, but insofar as they express the love of her little child, those nothings become most precious.

The lesson is obvious. We who desire in the spirit of little children to offer our lives to God as one continual act of humble and confident love can do so only through the little ordinary details which lie around us in our daily life. Unless we love Our Lord through "the toys, the pictures, the flowers" of everyday life, we shall never really love him at all. Again, as with the mother, so with our heavenly Father: he has no need of anything we offer him, but he wants us to go on offering things because he wants the love that lies behind them. For this reason the little things we do for him, in themselves apparently so insignificant, are to him infinitely precious. "You know well, Céline," says St. Thérèse in one of her letters, "that Our Lord does not look so much at the greatness of our actions, or even at their difficulty, as at the love with which we do them." [1]

It was her profound realization of the supernatural value

[1] *Autobiography*, p. 334.

of every detail of her ordinary life which made St. Thérèse the great Saint that she was, and it is that which today makes her beloved by ordinary people. During her last illness she said: "I want to point out to souls the means that I have always found so successful, to tell them that there is only one thing to do here below—to offer Our Lord the flowers of little sacrifices and win Him by our caresses. That is how I have won Him and that is why I shall be made so welcome." [2] In those words she teaches us that the wearying details in the humdrum routine of life are planned by our heavenly Father, to give us the means of offering ourselves to his Merciful Love and thus becoming saints. So far from looking upon these apparently insignificant details as burdens, and sighing for the far-off day when, released from them, we shall enjoy the peace and happiness of heaven, we are to see in them the very means by which heaven with its peace and happiness can be brought to us here and now. Thus the very secret of St. Thérèse's sanctity, so far from separating her from us, brings her into our midst, for the material of that sanctity was just the ordinary material which goes to make up the life of each one of us. Everything, even the smallest detail, can have an eternal significance, if done for love.

St. Thérèse insistently recommends this practice to others. "If you wish to be a Saint—and it will not be hard—keep only one end in view, always to do everything in order to please Jesus." [3] The simplicity of that programme and the very phraseology—always to do everything in order to please Jesus—make us hesitate: we sense the sentimental, and we would have expected something more virile, more heroic. But Our Lord himself said something very much the same. His Gospel was not sentimental; it lacked neither virility nor

[2] Ibid., p. 232.
[3] Ibid., p. 365.

heroism: *He hath not left me alone. For I do always the things that please him.*[4]

The theologian tells us to relate all things to our last end, but not everybody listens. St. Thérèse says, Do all things to please Jesus, and shows us how it is done, and in the doing of it she talks our language and lives our life, and the whole world goes after her.

Men and women learn most easily by pictures or by examples, and that surely was the divine method of teaching. The Incarnation was a living reality before it found its way into a theological treatise, and it is in parables and stories taken directly from human life that the Gospel is enshrined. True to Our Lord's method, St. Thérèse wrote no treatise; but she wrote the story of her life, and in that story we find all the fundamentals of the spiritual life portrayed in such a way that all can see and understand.

Let us then observe St. Thérèse and see how she herself followed the Little Way, the way of little things. She tells us, as we have seen, that there is only one thing to do here below, namely, to offer to Our Lord the flowers of small sacrifices. At first sight this seems more poetical than practical, but if we examine it we shall find that St. Thérèse is quite relentless in her realism. The seed-ground of these "flowers" is our everyday life. Consider for instance the passage in which she tells us quite explicitly what those flowers are. "To strew flowers is the only means I have of showing my love. That is to say I will let no little sacrifice escape me, not a look, not a word. I will make use of the smallest actions and I will do them all for love."[5] Here indeed is a comprehensive programme, yet one which is well within the scope of each one of us. Let us examine it in detail.

[4] Jn 8:29.
[5] *Autobiography*, p. 205.

a. *I will let no little sacrifice escape me*

We all try to escape little sacrifices, and we find we cannot do so: hence that inner conflict which makes us depressed and nervy and sick at heart. We are conscious of continual calls to a higher standard of spiritual life, of invitations to be less indulgent of ourselves and of our personal comfort, to be more disciplined in the use of our time, to be less subservient to human respect, and therefore to be less worldly. These are calls to make little sacrifices, and so they are painful to our human nature, and the immediate suffering obscures the ultimate spiritual gain. We are afraid, and we fail to respond.

At other times the occasions are provided by calls on our time through the interruptions of others, interruptions sometimes unavoidable but sometimes quite unnecessary; the call to sacrifice our own point of view where no principle is involved, for the sake of peace; the failure of the hopes we had placed in others; their lack of gratitude and lack of response; the spoiling by other people's mistakes or lack of vision of what we imagine God's plan to be. From such occasions as these there is no escape; we have to accept them in one way or another, and more often than not we do so in the wrong way. Knowing that they are going to hurt our self-love, we instinctively try to protect ourselves by making them minister to it. We let them rankle in our minds, wrap ourselves up in a garment of self-pity, and become irritable and discontented.

From all this St. Thérèse liberates us. She shows us that these occasions of sacrifice, so far from being something to be avoided, are providentially arranged by Our Lord and carefully proportioned by him to our powers; they are opportunities which we can grasp to prove our love and so give him joy. In her *Autobiography* she lets us see the simplicity of the incidents through which she herself grew in sanctity.

For a long time my place at meditation was near a Sister who fidgeted incessantly, either with her rosary or with something else. Possibly I alone heard her because of my very sensitive ear, but I cannot tell you to what extent I was tried by the irritating noise. There was a strong temptation to turn round and with one glance to silence the offender; yet in my heart I knew I ought to bear with her patiently, for the love of God first of all, and also to avoid causing her pain. I therefore remained quiet, but the effort cost me so much that sometimes I was bathed in perspiration, and my meditation consisted merely in the prayer of suffering. Finally I sought a way of gaining peace, in my inmost heart at least, and so I tried to find pleasure in the disagreeable noise. Instead of vainly trying not to hear it, I set myself to listen attentively as though it were delightful music, and my meditation—which was not the prayer of "quiet"—was passed in offering this music to Our Lord.

On another occasion when I was engaged in the laundry, the Sister opposite to me, who was washing handkerchiefs, kept splashing me continually with dirty water. My first impulse was to draw back and wipe my face in order to show her that I wanted her to be more careful. The next moment, however, I saw the folly of refusing treasures thus generously offered, and I carefully refrained from betraying any annoyance. On the contrary I made such efforts to welcome the shower of dirty water that at the end of half an hour I had taken quite a fancy to the novel kind of aspersion, and resolved to return as often as possible to the place where such precious treasures were freely bestowed.

You see, Mother, that I am but a very little soul, who can offer to God only very little things. It still happens that I frequently miss the opportunity of welcoming these small sacrifices which bring so much peace; but I am not discouraged—I bear the loss of a little peace and I try to be more watchful in the future.[6]

b. *Not a look*

Having shown us that she became a saint by offering every little daily sacrifice to Our Lord to give him joy and as an expression of her love for him, St. Thérèse then shows us how this works out in two most important aspects of our daily life— our looks and our words. "I will let no little sacrifice escape me, not a look." Few of us realize the importance of the expression on our faces. It gives us away long before we speak and often completely contradicts what we are saying. We can make a whole room cheerful by our faces, and by our expression we can cast gloom over the whole house. But to be always cheerful and smiling when we feel ill in body and sick at heart, and depressed with ourselves and disappointed with others, is most difficult, and for that reason it is one of the most important things in the spiritual life. St. Thérèse realized that, and so she tried to meet everybody and everything with a smile. In her portraits and statues she is usually depicted as smiling. Some critics regard this as forced and superficial; but it is in fact they who are superficial, for they have not learned that an essential point in sanctity is its gaiety. If people cannot picture us as always smiling, it is not because we are profound, but precisely because we are not profound enough. There is no such thing as a depressing saint. *Un saint triste est un triste saint*, says St. Francis de Sales. The secret of St. Thérèse's smile is to be found in a passage of her *Autobiography* where she deals with a novice whom she found depressed and in tears. "You ought not", St. Thérèse told her, "to allow your worries to

[6] Ibid., pp. 186–87.

be noticed by others, for nothing makes community life more trying than unevenness of temper." The novice replied: "You are right; henceforth I will keep my worries and tears for God alone."

> Tears for God! [promptly replied St. Thérèse]. That would never do. Far less to Him than to His creatures ought you to show a mournful face. He comes to our cloisters in search of rest—to forget the unceasing complaints of His friends in the world, who, instead of appreciating the value of the Cross, receive it more often than not with moans and tears. Frankly, this is not disinterested love. . . . It is for us to console Our Lord, and not for Him to be always consoling us. . . . Our Lord loves the glad of heart, the children that greet Him with a smile. When will you learn to hide your troubles from Him, or to tell Him gaily that you are happy to suffer for Him? The face is the mirror of the soul, and yours, like that of a contented little child, should always be calm and serene. Even when alone be cheerful, remembering always that you are in the sight of the Angels.[7]

In that passage the secret stands revealed. It is only those souls who, through an intimate personal communion with Our Lord, have come to appreciate fully the value of the Cross and are able to tell him gaily that they are happy to suffer with him—it is only those who will be able to meet everything and everybody around them with a smile.

It was this that gave to St. Thérèse's smile its invincible power in just those situations which seem so ordinary and which are yet so important.

> Formerly [she tells us], a holy nun of our community was a constant source of annoyance to me. Unwilling to yield to my natural antipathy, I prayed for her whenever I met

[7] Ibid., p. 304.

her. I tried also to render her as many services as I could, and when tempted to make a disagreeable answer, I made haste to smile and change the subject of conversation. The outcome was that one day, with a beaming countenance, she said: "Tell me, Sister Thérèse, what is it that attracts you to me so strongly? I never meet you without being welcomed with your most gracious smile." [8]

Again, in ministering to old Sister St. Pierre in a very difficult and trying routine, evening after evening, it was St. Thérèse's smile which ultimately won the confidence of the poor old invalid whom nobody else had been able to please. No wonder the Sisters said: "We shall have no fun today because Sister Thérèse is not coming to recreation." [9] In all this she had but one motive—to please Our Lord—and it was that which gave her her unique charm. "I look", she says, "for little opportunities, for the smallest trifles, to give pleasure to Jesus: a smile or a kind word, for instance, when I wish to be silent or to show that I am bored." [10]

Nothing less than the purely supernatural desire of pleasing Jesus will enable us to smile in the midst of trouble. Without this motive, it is too difficult: nothing else cuts at our self-love so deeply, for we not only have to make the sacrifice of hiding our troubles, but we also receive neither sympathy nor consolation from those around us. We get no credit for our efforts: people merely think we have no troubles at all! This brings us to the root of all depression and sadness, namely, pride and self-love. In our pride we try to bear our crosses more or less independently of Our Lord, and when we fail, we show our sadness in order that the consolation of others may feed our self-love. Clearly therefore it is those who try

[8] Ibid., p. 168.
[9] Ibid., p. 327.
[10] Ibid., p. 345.

to live lives of humble, confident love—that is to say, those who possess the spirit of childhood—who will see in this particular sacrifice flowers most worth plucking in order to give pleasure to Our Lord. "Our Lord loves the children who greet Him with a smile. Our face, like that of a contented little child, should always be calm and serene." It was the smile of Our Lady that charmed the soul of Bernadette. It was Our Lady's smile that cured little Thérèse. The true children of our heavenly Father, and of Mary, should always be recognizable by their smile. *God loveth a cheerful giver.*[11]

c. Not a word

The second fact in our ordinary life which St. Thérèse notes as specially giving us opportunities for little sacrifices, and as being therefore a precious means of sanctification, is our tongue. "I will let no little sacrifice escape me, not a look, not a word." The tongue and its activities! Here is a subject so vast that we can only indicate the lines pointed out to us by St. Thérèse.

In a letter to Mother Agnes she says: "Your letter has done me such good. The sentence, 'Let us refrain from saying a word which could raise us in the esteem of others', has indeed enlightened my soul. Yes, we must keep all for Jesus with jealous care. It is so good to work for Him alone." [12] Here at once is something which strikes home to each one of us. We all know the temptation to talk about everything we do in such a way that it is not the glory of God which is being served, but our own self-love. It is easy to talk incessantly about what we have done and how we did it; but it does no good to others, for it does not edify; and it does no good to us, for it

[11] 2 Cor 9:7.
[12] *Autobiography*, p. 354.

is centred in self. This use of the tongue for self-glorification is so subtle, and finds expression in so many ways, that the only safe course is to offer to Our Lord the sacrifice of never speaking of ourselves at all. "We must keep all for Jesus with jealous care." Our life and our works belong to him, and our life must be hid with Christ in God.

Closely allied to self-glorification in success is self-justification in failure. One of our deepest instincts is to excuse ourselves when things go wrong, even when it is our fault: still more ready are we to do so when the fault is not our own. As usual St. Thérèse goes straight to the point.

> What benefit do we derive from defending ourselves? Leave things as they are and say nothing. It is so sweet to allow ourselves to be judged anyhow, rightly or wrongly. It is not written in the Gospel that St. Mary Magdalen put forth excuses when charged by her sister with sitting idle at Our Lord's feet. She did not say: "Martha, if you knew the happiness that is mine and if you heard the words that I hear, you too would leave everything to share my joy and repose." No, she preferred to keep silent. Blessed silence which gives such peace to the soul.[13]

We know in our hearts that this is true, but in practice we argue that we are only standing up for our rights; we make great play with the fact that it is only justice after all and that justice is a virtue. And yet, except in the very rare cases where some principle is involved, we always lose by it, nobody is edified, and we do not even find the peace we sought. The infallible test is that there is no peace in our souls; and this is so precisely because we cannot make the slight sacrifice of self-love required. We cannot see that here is a flower, a little sacrifice, to be offered to Our Lord.

[13] Ibid., p. 312.

A very vivid passage in the *Autobiography* shows us St. Thérèse putting this into practice in one of those trivial instances which make up daily life.

> For several days you had been ill with bronchitis, and we were all very anxious. One morning in discharge of my office of sacristan I entered your infirmary, very gently, to put back the keys of the Communion grille. Though I took good care not to show it, I was inwardly rejoicing at the opportunity of seeing you. One of the Sisters, however, feared that I should wake you, and discreetly wished to take the keys from me. I told her, with all possible politeness, that I was as anxious as she that there should be no noise, adding that it was my duty to return them. I see now that it would have been more perfect to yield, but I did not think so then, and consequently tried to enter the room. What she feared came to pass—the noise we made woke you, and the blame was cast upon me. The Sister made a lengthy discourse, the point of which was that I was the guilty person. I was burning to defend myself when happily it occurred to me that if I began to do so, I should certainly lose my peace of mind, and that as I had not sufficient virtue to keep silence when accused, my only chance of safety lay in flight. No sooner thought than done, and I fled. ... But my heart beat so violently that I could not go far and had to sit down on the stairs to taste in peace and quiet the fruits of my victory.[14]

If in our conversation we seek to avoid all self-centredness we shall have more time to think of others and so to see their point of view. Thus we shall be the last to criticize or impute motives. If we leap to criticize others, it merely indicates that we do not know our own failings, for a sure sign of a realization of our own faults is tenderness towards those of others.

[14] Ibid., p. 169.

"It is not playing the game to argue with a Sister that she is in the wrong, even when it is true, because we are not answerable for her conduct. We must not be Justices of the Peace, but Angels of peace only."[15]

Self-forgetfulness in conversation is a blessed thing in many other ways. It will, for example, enable us to get out of ourselves and enter into the interests of others.

> When I am talking to a novice I am ever on the watch to mortify myself, avoiding all questions which would tend to gratify my curiosity. Should she begin to speak on an interesting subject, and, leaving it unfinished, pass on to another that wearies me, I am careful not to remind her of the digression, for no good can come of self-seeking.[16]

To be interested in the concerns of others enriches us beyond all conception; but it involves sacrifice, and for that reason we often fail to experience its blessedness. Above all, self-forgetfulness in conversation develops in us the gift of noticing at once when someone else is in need of consolation or encouragement. We are continually in contact with other people, and often just at the moment when a little interest, a word of understanding, of consolation, or of encouragement would mean everything to them. The capacity to say that word is one of the greatest gifts in ordinary daily life. We possess that gift exactly in proportion as we forget ourselves and make the sacrifice which self-forgetfulness in our daily conversation demands. To do this continually requires a high degree of love of Our Lord. Nothing less than that will carry us through, for only too often our efforts will go unrewarded.

> It frequently needs only a word or a smile to impart fresh life to a despondent soul. Yet it is not merely in the hope

[15] Ibid., p. 312.
[16] Ibid., p. 177.

of bringing consolation that I wish to be kind; if it were so, I should soon be discouraged, for often well-intentioned words are totally misunderstood. Consequently, in order that I may lose neither time nor labour, I try to act solely to please Our Lord.[17]

d. *I will make use of the smallest actions,*
and I will do them all for love

Finally, St. Thérèse gathers in every single action and incident in human life and claims it for Our Lord. "Jesus tells us that the smallest actions done for His love are those which charm His Heart. If it were necessary to do great things, we should be deserving of pity, but we are fortunate indeed, since Jesus lets Himself be led captive by the smallest action."[18]

St. Thérèse does not say the small actions, but the smallest. It is not difficult to see, in theory, the place which small sacrifices hold in the spiritual life, even though it is not easy to put this into practice; but that the smallest actions of every day, those which are apparently the most indifferent, can be directly related to Our Lord and become a means by which we show our love to him; that they can be made channels of grace to our souls, and that by them earth can be directly linked with heaven—that, for most of us, is very difficult to grasp.

What did she mean by "smallest action"? She gives us an example. "I endeavoured," she says, "above all, to practise little hidden acts of virtue, such as folding the mantles which the Sisters had forgotten, and being on the alert to render them help."[19] *Folding the mantles which the Sisters had forgotten —that*

[17] Ibid., p. 183.
[18] Ibid., p. 364.
[19] Ibid., p. 133.

is what the smallest actions meant in the convent life of St. Thérèse. In our spiritual snobbery we smile at it as petty and trifling; it would have been more practical to make the Sisters do it themselves: but while the smile is still on our lips we begin to see that it was the coalescing of just such little actions as these, which produced the colossal phenomenon of St. Thérèse of the Child Jesus.

Many of us shrink from pushing this truth to its logical conclusion for fear that minute attention to detail will make us scrupulous. Surely—we argue—it is safer to make, at the Morning Offering, a virtual intention covering all the day, and then carry on with practical common sense.

This sounds excellent in theory, but too often it breaks down in practice and merely ends in the making of the Morning Offering, while we slip through the day on a purely natural plane till we arrive at our prayers in the evening; and it is precisely our habit of thus meeting the smallest actions of our daily life on the natural plane which makes them more than we can cope with. Divorced from their true purpose, that of leading us out of ourselves to God and to our fellow-men, they imprison us within ourselves and make us give way to self-pity and discontent.

On the other hand, if we do everything to please Our Lord we shall find ourselves becoming more and more alert to help others and far more conscious of the endless little opportunities around us, the value of which we had never realized before. To find time for a visit to Our Lord in the Blessed Sacrament will become perfectly easy, whereas before it required a superhuman effort. We shall be able to carry on happily through the midst of the smallest details of the day, because through them we have found the way out of ourselves into the heart of God and into the hearts of our fellow-men.

Thus liberated from the prison of self-love into the glorious liberty of the children of God, we love him and his will alone, regardless of the forms in which it comes to us, and we love others for his sake, regardless of the circumstances that may be involved. *Thou shalt love the Lord Thy God with thy whole heart... and thy neighbour as thyself:*[20] herein is perfect sanctity. That is what St. Thérèse means by becoming a victim of love, and she leads us to it through little things.

The supernatural value of the smallest details of human life is one of the most profound of the many lessons which St. Thérèse teaches us. That alone would justify the title "The Little Way", for it is pre-eminently the way of little things. "There is only one thing to do here below, namely to offer Our Lord the flowers of little sacrifices, to win Him by our caresses."[21] *Caresses*—she is right. Just as in human love it is the little attentions which betray the depth of human feelings, so it is our little actions done for love which show the intensity of our devotion to Our Lord.

The little is the key to the great, for good or for ill. Scripture tells us: *He that contemneth small things shall fall by little and little.*[22] It also tells us: *He that is faithful in that which is least is faithful also in that which is greater.*[23]

[20] Lk 10:27.
[21] *Autobiography*, p. 232.
[22] Ecclus. 19:1.
[23] Lk 16:10.

XII

SUFFERING (1)

SPIRITUAL CHILDHOOD, as we have seen, finds its practical expression in our offering to God, for love of him and our fellow-men, the ordinary details of our daily life, all of which are carefully chosen for us by our heavenly Father as the material of our sanctification. But what about suffering, pain, and death? Can those grim accompaniments of human life, which seem to quench our hope and dull our consciousness of the heavenly Father's love, can those be offered as expressions of our love for him and for those around us? Can they too tend to our sanctification, draw us into a closer union with God? If the Little Way can guide us here, it will indeed solve the deepest problem of human life, for we all have to suffer, and we all have to die.

To understand the light which the Little Way throws on the endurance of suffering, we must again begin by considering the natural order. What is it that takes a small child to its mother more quickly than anything else? Pain! The moment a child is hurt, far from trying to bear its pain alone or imagining that its mother has abandoned it, it runs straight to her arms, and there its pain, although not taken away, becomes easier to bear. In her arms, and through the consciousness of her love, the child receives from her something which she alone can give. Not only does the suffering lose its sting; it is the means of enfolding the child in a specially tender love that otherwise it could never know.

If we put this into the supernatural order and translate it into terms of St. Thérèse's teaching, the parallel is clear. As soon as anyone sets out to follow the Little Way, in a spirit of complete dependence on the love of God and with the wish to offer every detail of his life as an expression of his own love, he will soon come across pain. So far from trying to meet it in his own strength, or imagining that God has abandoned him, he immediately says: "My heavenly Father's love is somewhere in and behind this pain." In other words, the soul which is really childlike relates its suffering to its Father's love and at once throws itself into his arms, where it finds not only strength to endure but a depth and tenderness of love which can come to it only through suffering and which brings it very close to its crucified Lord.

The degree of that closeness will depend on how completely we surrender ourselves to the Father's embrace, and this in turn depends on how far we, through grace, are converted from our self-reliance and independence and, in face of the problem of suffering and pain, become as little children. In other words, when we meet with suffering—physical, mental, or spiritual—by practising the virtues of love, humility, and confidence, in the spirit of a very little child, we find ourselves drawn by that suffering into the companionship of our crucified Lord, and there learn by experience the inner meaning and purpose of the mystery of pain. It was precisely the fidelity with which St. Thérèse practised those virtues that united her so closely to her crucified Saviour and taught her the secrets of the love of God which are hidden from the wise and prudent and revealed only to little ones.

The first secret that she learned was the immense value of suffering. To her it was a treasure because Our Lord chose it for himself when he was upon earth. "Suffering", she writes, "puts great treasures within our reach. Indeed it is our very livelihood, and so precious that Jesus came down upon earth on purpose to possess it."[1]

It is only those who suffer who can really understand the amazing mystery that when God came into this world, he chose pain and suffering not only for himself but for his Mother, and however unfathomable, this mystery is the key to our own suffering. "Jesus", says St. Thérèse, writing to Céline about their father's mental illness, "in His immense love has chosen for us of all crosses the most precious.... How can we complain when He Himself has been considered as one struck by God and afflicted?"[2] "In this land of exile we meet with many a thorn and many a bitter plant, but is not this the portion which earth gave to our Divine Spouse? It is fitting, then, to consider good and most beautiful this same portion which has become our own."[3] In her poem to Our Lady she writes:

> Puisque le Roi des Cieux a voulu que sa Mère
> Fût soumise à la nuit, à l'angoisse du cœur
> Alors, c'est donc un bien de souffrir sur la terre.[4]

Between all friends there is a bond which binds them together and makes their friendship live. In our friendship with Our Blessed Lord that bond is suffering, for by it we learn that the mystery of suffering is a mystery of love. As lover looks into lover's eyes and is silent and understands, so the suffering soul, looking upon a suffering God, needs no explanation and

---

[1] *Autobiography*, p. 336.

[2] *Spirit of St. Thérèse*, comp. by the Carmelites of Lisieux (Burns and Oates), p. 98.

[3] Ibid., p. 99.

[4] "Since on the Blessed Maid who gave Him birth,/ Darkness and pain the King of Heaven bestowed,/ How great a good must suffering be on earth!"— "Pourquoi je t'aime, O Marie", *Poems*. Translated by D. A. P.

is at rest. But there are two sides to every friendship, and so in St. Thérèse's eyes the wonder was not merely that through her suffering she found a Friend in the Son of God, but that the Son of God found a friend in her. Suffering was offered to her that, through it, she might show a special delicacy of love to him and so enter into the inner circle of those who share his sorrows.

> He holds out His hand to receive an alms of love proved by suffering.... He wants to be able to say to us as to His apostles: *You are they who have continued with Me in temptations.* The temptations of Jesus—what a mystery! He too, then, has been tried. Yes, He has had his trials, and often He has trodden the winepress alone. *I looked for one that would grieve together with Me, but there was none: and for one that would comfort Me and I found none.*[5]

"We now share the chalice of His sufferings; but how sweet it will be to us one day to hear the gentle words: *You are they who have continued with Me in My temptations.*"[6]

Suffering then is the seal of the divine friendship. We are no longer alone: God is suffering for us and with us. To share in that friendship forged by suffering is the greatest treasure we can possess. "What a favour from Jesus! How He must love us to send us so great a sorrow! Eternity will not be long enough to thank Him for it. He heaps His favours upon us as upon the greatest Saints. What can be His loving designs for our souls?"[7] *I count all things but to be loss...that I may know him...and the fellowship of his sufferings.*[8] The fellowship of his sufferings! The intimate friendship of Jesus! To gain this, St. Thérèse, like St. Paul, would count all else well lost. We have

[5] *Spirit of St. Thérèse*, p. 101.
[6] *Autobiography*, p. 348.
[7] Ibid., p. 334.
[8] Phil 3:8–10.

seen that in one of her letters to her sister Céline she asks the question: "What can be His loving designs for our souls?" In another letter to the same sister she gives the answer: "Why does Jesus allow us to suffer?... Because He knows that it is the only means of preparing us to know Him as He knows Himself, and to become ourselves divine."[9] Fellowship becomes union; companionship merges into identity of life. If we are childlike enough to allow Our Lord to lead us by the hand unresistingly along the path of suffering, we shall find, as we unite our suffering with his, that it is no longer a matter of mere companionship, but that he is identified with us and we with him, and that he is living in us and suffering in us. *With Christ I am nailed to the cross. And I live, now not I: but Christ liveth in me.*[10]

Union with himself through the Cross of his beloved Son—such is our heavenly Father's design for our souls, and the means by which he will perfect his design are suffering and pain. "Let us be one with God even in this life; in order to be so, we should be more than resigned, we should embrace the Cross with joy."[11] To be more than resigned, to embrace the Cross with joy, that is exactly what we find so hard, though we know that the reward is union with God even in this life. What then was the secret that made it possible for St. Thérèse?

Little children have a way of penetrating through the accidental and the superficial and of getting to the heart of a question in a most disconcerting manner, in a way we grown-ups cannot do. It was so with St. Thérèse and the Cross. As she meditated upon the Crucifixion, she did not see it merely as an event in time, looking through time, she saw it as the design of God ordained before the foundation of the world, revealed

[9] *Autobiography*, p. 333.
[10] Gal 2:19–20.
[11] *Autobiography*, p. 335.

indeed in time, but existing from all eternity within the will of God. Over the crypt of the basilica at Lisieux are written these words: *I have loved thee with an everlasting love: therefore have I drawn thee, taking pity on thee.*[12] Those words are there because they were specially dear to St. Thérèse. They show us the proper setting of the Cross upon which Our Lord was lifted to draw all men to him—the eternal love and will of God. Meditating on those words, St. Thérèse, even in her worst sufferings, saw all the happenings of time as part of the eternal will of God and knew herself to be her heavenly Father's child, cradled in his everlasting arms.

Set in a world of time and space, tending always to make this world our home, when we come across suffering, pain, and death, we do indeed try to relate them to the Cross. But when we find that in this world of time the Cross does not apparently and immediately solve our problems as our earthbound judgment would expect, we become baffled and perplexed; and one of the reasons for this is that we tend to think of the Cross merely as an event in time. If we lose our perspective of eternity the problems of time take on a far greater proportion than they should; we lose our heads, and our crosses are all the harder to bear.

Though we would strenuously deny it if charged with it, we do in fact behave as if God himself had been taken off his guard by the Fall, as if he had not quite got the situation in hand. To be more than resigned, to embrace the Cross with joy, we must see it not as an emergency measure, but as part of the eternal rhythm of the invincible will of the Father, who ordains all things, even the most minute and insignificant, with fatherly love.

Let us consider afresh, then, the invincible will and love of

[12] Jer 31:3.

God, which in theory we know so well, but which in practice it is so hard to realize. *God created man incorruptible, and to the image of his own likeness he made him.*[13] When God created the human race he, their Father, created them to share his own life—as all children share their father's life—the life of supernatural love. They shared that life as long as they obeyed him, as again is the case with families on earth. Man was made in the image of his Father, and since God is a free spirit, therefore, man was created a free spirit, with an intellect and will of his own. So long as man obeyed his Father, his intellect and will, responsive to the Father's love, were able to control his lower faculties. Man was a harmony within himself, and all his social contacts with those around him were to be a harmony as well. There was no suffering, no pain, no sorrow, no death in the original plan, but all depended upon a free acceptance of the authority of the Father's love.

Then came the Fall. *By the envy of the devil, death came into the world.*[14] The devil, inspired by envy, tempted our first parents and they fell. The temptation to which they succumbed was a temptation to pride: *You shall be as Gods, knowing good and evil.*[15] In his desire to be self-sufficient and independent, Adam, by an act of disobedience, withdrew his intellect and will from his Father's loving control. By that act the human race, through Adam, its head, rejected God's fatherly commands and God's fatherly embrace and threw over the loving obedience of the creature to its Creator, of the child to its father. The moment the human race, through Adam, had thus rejected the Father's rule, the intellect and will, uncontrolled by the supernatural love of God, were unable to govern the lower faculties. Instead of a harmony within himself, man

[13] Wis 2:23.
[14] Wis 2:24.
[15] Gen 3:5.

found conflict, and from his divided self sprang all the sorrow, suffering, pain, and death in human life. Wherever he went, in all his social contacts, he carried his tragedy with him. Where there should have been peace and harmony there came suffering, pain, and death, and all owing to disobedience, a disobedience springing from pride in search of an imaginary independence of the Father's love.

Was God caught unawares, taken off his guard? That we know to be impossible. From all eternity God had foreseen the Fall and was to draw from it a good greater than that which Adam lost. He was to restore his children to a yet more intimate embrace. *When the fulness of the time was come, God sent his Son, made of a woman . . . that we might receive the adoption of sons.*[16] It might have been thought that there could be no closer union between man and God than the life of supernatural grace in which Adam had been created. But no, through union with the Sacred Humanity of the Second Person of the Holy Trinity, Our Lord Jesus Christ, God-made-Man, Almighty God was to restore man to a sonship more intimate still.

> When the entire human race had fallen in its first parents, God in His mercy willed in such a manner to bring succour through His only-begotten Son Jesus Christ to the creature made in His own image, that its second state should excel beyond the dignity of its original state. Happy if it had not fallen from what God made it, but happier if it remain in what He has re-made.[17]

In the words of St. Paul, *But not as the offence, so also the gift. For if by the offence of one, many died: much more the grace of God . . . hath abounded unto many. . . . And where sin abounded, grace did more abound.*[18] It is the teaching of St. Thomas that if man had

[16] Gal 4:4–5.
[17] St. Leo the Great, *Sermo* 72, c. II.
[18] Rom 5:15, 20.

not fallen, the eternal Word would not have become Incarnate.[19] That is Catholic tradition. "For if flesh had not needed
to be saved, in no wise would the Word of God have become
flesh." [20] "The Word would by no means have been made
Man, unless the need of man had been the cause thereof." [21]
"If man had not perished, the Son of Man would not have
come." [22] All this is beautifully expressed in the cry of the
Church: "*O Felix Culpa!* O happy fault, that has won for us
so loving and so mighty a Redeemer." Bethlehem, then, is the
first unfolding in time of the eternal plan of God's merciful
love, for the restoration of his children.

> The character of the Incarnation is intrinsically one of
> mercy. Had man not fallen, God would indeed have loved
> him as he loves the angels, but he would not strictly have
> shown him mercy. The Incarnation has the character of a
> mother's pity for her child who has tumbled and hurt him-
> self. She loved him before, but never so much as she does
> now. The caresses which she now lavishes upon him would
> have been mere extravagance before; now they are the
> spontaneous over-flowing of a heart whose flood-gates
> have been opened.[23]

It was precisely that revelation of the Merciful Love of God
stooping down to Bethlehem and becoming a little child in
order to restore his erring children to his embrace that was
the dominating devotion of St. Thérèse of the Child Jesus. "To
me He has especially manifested His infinite mercy, and in this

[19] *Summa theologiae*, III, q. 1, art. 3.

[20] Irenaeus, *Adversus haereses*, l. 5, c. 14, n. 1.

[21] Athanasius, *Oratio 2 contra Arianos*, n. 56.

[22] Augustine, *Sermo* 174, c. 2.

[23] Dom Bruno Webb, O.S.B., *Why Does God Permit Evil?* (Burns and Oates),
p. 60. An excellent treatment of this subject. It is from this work that this particular grouping of quotations from the Fathers has been taken, with the kind
permission of the author.

mirror I contemplate all His other attributes. There each appears radiant with love." [24]

The plan of the Merciful Love which unfolds at Bethlehem, moves irresistibly to the Cross for its fulfilment. Bethlehem and Calvary are inseparable. *Wherefore, when he cometh into the world he saith: Sacrifice and oblation thou wouldst not: but a body thou hast fitted to me. Holocausts for sin did not please thee. ... Then said I: Behold, I come to do thy will, O God.*[25] Just as the central factor of man's Fall was an act of disobedience, so the central factor of man's Redemption was an act of obedience, offered in our human nature by the Son of God himself. *As by the disobedience of one man, many were made sinners: so also by the obedience of one, many shall be made just.*[26]

Moreover, as the act of disobedience by which the children were separated from their heavenly Father brought in its train sorrow, suffering, pain, and death, the act of obedience, which makes them just again, had to be accomplished in the midst of that sorrow, suffering, pain, and death. These stages of man's journey away from his Father's love become the stepping-stones of his return. By sharing our suffering, by living our life side by side with us, Our Lord enables us to sanctify it all.

Suffering is the result of sin, and suffering is the price of sin; Calvary is the scene of reconciliation of the Father with his children. *It hath well pleased the Father ... through him to reconcile all things unto himself, making peace through the blood of his cross.*[27] And it is the scene of reconciliation, because Our Lord, who did not have to die, did in fact will to die, to die for us "propter nos homines". *Because the children are partak-*

[24] *Autobiography*, p. 147.
[25] Heb 10:5–6, 9.
[26] Rom 5:19.
[27] Col 1:19–20.

ers of flesh and blood, he also himself in like manner hath been par-
taker of the same: that, through death, he might destroy him who
had the empire of death, that is to say, the devil: and might deliver
them who through the fear of death were all their lifetime subject to
servitude.[28]

He became Man for us. He lived for us, and he knew from
eternity what he would do *propter nos homines.* To each of us
St. Peter says: *You were redeemed with the precious blood of Christ,*
as of a lamb unspotted and undefiled, foreknown indeed before the
foundation of the world.[29]

To be united with that divine plan fore-ordained from all
eternity, to be nailed to the Cross with Christ so that she lived,
yet not she but Christ lived in her, to be thus identified with
him on his Cross and in his Resurrection—that, for St.
Thérèse, summed up her whole vocation.

She was not jolted or jarred along the way of the Cross,
perplexed and stumbling in the dark; she met every cross with
joy because she saw it in its true setting; she looked beyond it
to the love of her Father from whom it came and to whom
it led; she saw it in the setting of eternity. "Time is but a
shadow, a dream. Already God sees us in glory, He rejoices in
our eternal happiness. How this thought sustains my soul! I
understand then why He lets us suffer."[30]

Her vision was not bounded by time. Looking forward, she
knew that *the sufferings of this time are not worthy to be compared*
with the glory to come that shall be revealed in us.[31] Looking back-
ward she knew with equal certainty that, just as the Cross was
ordained before the foundation of the world, so she was chosen in him before the foundation of the world; she knew that

[28] Heb 2:14–15.
[29] 1 Pet 1:19–20.
[30] *Spirit of St. Thérèse*, p. 98.
[31] Rom 8:18.

in him she was predestined by her heavenly Father to the adoption of children—to Spiritual Childhood.

In order to cooperate with this divine plan, she offered herself to all the suffering that came in her path, that through it the Merciful Love of God might do its work in her, that, delivered from all self-love and pride, she might be perfectly united to her Saviour. "Suffering united to love is the only thing which appears to me desirable in this valley of tears." [32]

Finally, because she was such a little child and, as she said, "capable of only very little things", St. Thérèse saw that the application of the divine plan lay, not in preparing herself for some glorious martyrdom in the far distant future, but in the loving acceptance of the little daily sufferings that lie immediately to hand. "Why are you so gay today?" she was asked during her last illness. She replied: "Because this morning I have had two little trials. Nothing gives me little joys like little trials." [33] Here once again she joins hands with us. We all have little trials; sometimes in fact our life appears to be almost entirely made up of them. To lift these small humiliating drudgeries of human life out of their prosaic dullness, by seeing them as God's chosen means for the fullest union with him here and now in this life, and, seeing them thus, to accept them with joy, this is to rob all suffering of its sting and to establish the soul in peace and joy. The Little Way is made perfect through little sufferings lovingly accepted for the love of God.

---

[32] *Autobiography*, p. 374.

[33] *Novissima verba*, comp. by the Carmelites of Lisieux (Burns and Oates), May 19.

XIII

SUFFERING (2)

THE PARTICULAR characteristic of St. Thérèse as a guide of souls lies not so much in the fact that she teaches us the most profound truths of the spiritual life —this indeed she does—as in the fact that she illustrated them in practice in her own life and recorded that life in a setting of the simplest character and in words easily understood by all. The *Autobiography* is the spiritual life personified. We will now consider how her teaching as to the place that suffering holds in the Little Way of Spiritual Childhood finds expression in the story of her life.

From the very first, St. Thérèse's life was one of suffering. "As I was to be the spouse of Our Lord at so tender an age, it was necessary that I should suffer from childhood." [1] Suffering first came to little Thérèse with the loss of her mother when she was only four and a half years old. "With my mother's death", she writes, "began the second period of my life, the most sorrowful of all, especially after you, my little Mother [her sister Pauline], had entered Carmel." [2] The death of her mother was a shattering blow. Thérèse lost much of her gaiety, was driven in upon herself, and became sensitive and silent. Less than four years later, before she had been able to recover from that blow, she saw Pauline, who had taken her mother's

[1] *Autobiography*, p. 41.
[2] Ibid., p. 43.

place, leave home herself to enter Carmel. "In a flash," she says, "I beheld life as it really is, full of suffering and constant partings, and I shed most bitter tears. At that time the joy of sacrifice was still unknown to me." [3] At first, then, suffering seems to have been to St. Thérèse just suffering, stark and naked, as indeed it so often appears to most of us; but, three years later, soon after her First Communion, it was very different.

> Once in preparing me for my Communion my sister Marie spoke of suffering, and said that in all probability, instead of making me walk by that road, God, in His goodness, would carry me always like a little child. The following day, after Communion, these words came back to me, bringing with them an ardent desire for suffering, as well as a conviction that I should have many a cross to bear. Then a wave of consolation swept over my soul. Suffering became my treasure; I found in it charms that held me spellbound, though as yet I did not appreciate it to the full. [4]

Her conviction was prophetic. Almighty God, just because he was her Father and she so truly his little child, was indeed going to carry her in his arms, not away from suffering but into it and through it, right to her home in heaven. When she was still only a girl of fifteen Thérèse entered Carmel. In the description of her entry we see how this mysterious blend of peace and joy with great suffering had become still more firmly established. She describes with what suffering she said good-bye to her father and sisters and how the door closed upon her. Then she continues:

> My desire was now accomplished, and my soul was filled with so deep a peace that it baffles all attempt at descrip-

[3] Ibid., p. 59.
[4] Ibid., p. 76.

tion. This peace has been my portion during the eight and a half years of my life within these walls, never forsaking me even amid the hardest trials. Suffering opened wide her arms to me from the very first, and I took her fondly to my heart.... Unknown to anyone this was the path I trod for fully five years.[5]

At this point we inevitably ask ourselves what it was that enabled St. Thérèse, at the age of fifteen, to realize completely how precious suffering is and thus to grasp the central secret of sanctity, which we, so much older, find so very hard to learn. The answer lies in her vivid sense of the eternal. She saw everything *sub specie aeternitatis*. Usually that consciousness of the eternal is made real to us only through the inadequacy of this world of time, brought home to us through sickness, failure, or the loss of someone we love. St. Thérèse's sense of the eternal, and of the consequent transitoriness of this life, was with her from the very first in a quite extraordinary degree. With the death of her mother this world became less than ever her home: this world with its sorrows and its joys was but a broken fleeting thing which had no meaning apart from heaven.

Suffering and sadness have now entered into the life of little Thérèse, and although, as we have seen, she suffered intensely, and temporarily lost much of that gaiety which later she was completely to regain, yet, deep down in her soul, suffering is doing its appointed work by turning her thoughts more than ever from earth to heaven, and by developing her soul in prayer.

Henceforth suffering becomes for her inseparable from its background of heaven and the love of her Father who is in heaven. Almighty God's eternal plan of restoring his children

[5] Ibid., p. 121.

to himself through suffering is beginning to be realized in
Thérèse at the age of seven. That understanding develops from
then onwards with amazing rapidity. At the age of thirteen she
left school, and, only three years later, while still a novice in
Carmel, she writes, in a letter to her sister Céline, words
which, in view of her sixteen years, must surely rank among
the most remarkable in the history of the saints: "I find only
one joy, that of suffering, and this joy, which is not a pleasure
of the senses, is above all joy. Life is passing and eternity
drawing nearer. Soon we shall live the very life of God." [6]
Looking at life from the standpoint of eternity, she was not
overwhelmed by this world's sufferings; she did not see them
merely as happenings in time—disjointed, jarring, apparently
purposeless, and therefore often almost more than she could
bear—but as the greatest possible treasure, to be accepted with
joy as being the means specially chosen by Almighty God
whereby his children should be made perfect in love, reunited
to their Father in their home in heaven, and, in the Saint's own
words, "live the very life of God".

Let us not imagine for a moment that those words were
the ecstatic utterance of a novice in her first fervour; on the
contrary, they were written in the midst of the most acute sorrow. Thérèse's father was seized with a paralysis which gradually deprived him of all his faculties, including his reason. She
loved her father more than anyone else in the world, and this
suffering cost her many tears, for it penetrated her sensitive
nature to its very depths. Never for a moment, however, did
she lose her inmost peace or feel herself abandoned by her
heavenly Father; on the contrary, it was to her the mark of
God's special love for her. "I cannot fathom the infinite love
which has led Our Lord to treat us in this way. Our dear Father

[6] Ibid., p. 335.

must indeed be loved by God to have so much suffering given to him." [7] All is seen in the light of eternity.

Suffering, then, is the supreme expression of her heavenly Father's love for her, because it is his chosen means of making her one with him in supernatural love. The loving acceptance of suffering, therefore, and a joyous surrender to it because through it her heavenly Father works out his design for her soul—this with inexorable logic becomes in turn the supreme expression of her love for him. She will offer herself to be the joyous victim of his Merciful Love.

> *Sous le pressoir de la souffrance*
> *Je te prouverai mon amour.*
> *Je ne veux d'autre jouissance*
> *Que de m'immoler chaque jour.* [8]

In suffering she found the means of "loving Jesus even unto folly" as he had loved her, of satisfying her insatiable longing "to die the death of love" as Jesus had died for her upon the Cross. [9]

Further, since suffering is the chosen means of union with God, it is for Thérèse the beginning of glory here and now. Suffering was the condition of Our Blessed Lord's glory. *Ought not Christ to have suffered these things and so to enter into his glory?* [10] So it shall be with her: her sufferings are, to her, the beginning of that eternal glory which the Father had ordained for her through the sufferings of his most beloved Son and for which she had been predestined before ever the

---

[7] Ibid.

[8] "Crushed by a heavy load of suffering/ As grapes are crushed ere they be turned to wine,/ Let me thus prove my love. Let this one thing,/ The joy of daily sacrifice, be mine."—"Mes désirs près du Tabernacle", *Poems*. Translated by D. A. P.

[9] *Autobiography*, p. 240.

[10] Lk 24:26.

world was made. "Time is but a shadow, a dream. Already God sees us in glory, He rejoices in our eternal happiness. . . . How this thought sustains my soul. I understand then why He lets us suffer." [11]

It is important that we should pause here for a moment, for there will be some who feel that all this is beyond them; the very language is becoming too much like that of the great mystics. Clearly St. Thérèse was given a very special grace not granted to us. We can indeed trace the lines upon which her soul developed in its realization of the rôle of suffering, and we can admire their beauty, but for us it remains but a vision, an ideal. We are conscious of a growing gulf between us and the Saint: we can see no point of contact whereby we can put this into practice. How, we ask ourselves, can all this be expressed in our everyday life?

It is true that St. Thérèse had a very special grace, apt for her very special vocation, but the vital point lies not in the fact of that grace but in the fact of her cooperation with it, and that cooperation was fulfilled through the medium of the ordinary sufferings of life. There is our point of contact. It lies in the last two words of the poem we have quoted above— "chaque jour". Everyday life with its sufferings—her mother's death, the separation from her sisters as, one after the other, they entered Carmel, her father's tragic illness, misunderstandings and sufferings of every kind in the daily routine of her convent life—those were the medium through which she cooperated with the grace of her vocation.

Further, the power which enabled her thus to cooperate was that gift of supernatural grace which is common to us all, which the Church plants in our soul at Baptism, and by which we become the children of God, sharing his very life. In other

[11] *Autobiography*, p. 338.

words, it was the grace of Spiritual Childhood—and here
again we are on common ground with her. We are all children of God, and heaven, not this world, is our home: we are
all immortal souls destined for a supernatural end. Moreover,
since these immortal souls of ours are enshrined in finite
human bodies, therefore every detail of our human life
within us, and all our contacts with people and things around
us, are charged with the supernatural and are related to our
last end, as the means by which we are to be made perfect in
supernatural love and so prepared for our home in heaven. As
a result of the Fall, this restoration to union with God through
supernatural love, this loving obedience to the will of God—
for obedience is ever the core of love—has to be wrought out
in a human nature prone to disobedience and in a world alien-
ated from God. It follows, then, that this work of restoration
can be accomplished only by suffering; only with pain can the
will learn to go the way of God's will and not the way of its
own all but mastering inclination.

It was so with Our Lord. *Whereas indeed he was the Son of
God, he learned obedience by the things which he suffered. And being
consummated, he became, to all that obey him, the cause of eternal
salvation.*[12] Again, *It became him for whom are all things, who had
brought many children into glory, to perfect the author of their salvation, by his passion.*[13] As it was with the Author of their salvation, so it must be with each of the children thus brought to
glory: as it was with the Head of the Mystical Body, so must
it be with every individual member of that Body. It is by the
loving acceptance of the sufferings that come to us in our daily
life, and by the joyful uniting of them with those of Our
Blessed Lord upon the Cross, it is by that alone that we are
made one with Almighty God, and by that alone is Almighty

[12] Heb 5:8–9.
[13] Heb 2:10.

God's work of supernatural love perfected in our souls. There is no other way: *If any man will come after me, let him deny himself and take up his cross and follow me.*[14]

To offer ourselves as victims of the Merciful Love as it purifies our soul through suffering, that is our daily vocation: to die the death of love with Jesus on the Cross, to that we are pledged. There is nothing new or extreme here. It is merely that the clarity, the simplicity, the directness of St. Thérèse's language lights up our ordinary vocation afresh, and we, who thought we saw, find that we have never really seen and are embarrassed.

Thus far we have been considering St. Thérèse as she met with the sufferings of everyday life coming to her in her home, at her school, and during her first years in Carmel. All the writings and all the incidents so far noted, incredible though it may seem, come from her life before she was seventeen. For the next five years she continued thus, but it is the last eighteen months of her life that are about to claim our attention. We are now to follow her along that path of special suffering by which Almighty God took her to himself by the way of the Cross and perfected in her that act of love which she so desired to offer him. We shall see how, safe in her Father's arms, she moves serenely along the road of physical pain and spiritual desolation, and how at last, through death, she enters into life. The first warning came in the early morning of Good Friday, April 3, 1896. She tells the story with characteristic simplicity:

> In the early hours of Good Friday—how precious the memory of it is to me!—Jesus gave me the hope that I should soon join Him in His beautiful heaven. Not having obtained permission to watch at the Altar of Repose

[14] Mt 16:24.

throughout Thursday night, I returned to our cell at midnight. Scarcely had I laid my head on the pillow when I felt a hot stream rise to my lips, and thinking I was going to die, my heart was overwhelmed with joy. I had already put out our lamp, so I mortified my curiosity till morning and went peacefully to sleep. At five o'clock, the time for rising, I remembered immediately that I had some good news to learn, and going to the window I found, as I had expected, that our handkerchief was saturated with blood. What hope filled my heart! I was firmly convinced that on the anniversary of His death my Beloved had allowed me to hear His first call, like a sweet distant murmur heralding His approach.... On this Good Friday I shared in all the austerities of Carmel without any relaxation. Never had they seemed so consoling, the hope of soon entering heaven filled me with joy. When I returned to our cell in the evening of that happy day, I was still full of joy and I was quietly falling asleep when, as on the previous night, Jesus gave me the same sign of my speedy entrance into eternal life. My faith at this time was so clear and so lively that the thought of heaven was my greatest delight.... But during the Paschal days, that time so full of light, Our Lord allowed my soul to be plunged in thickest gloom, and the thought of heaven, so sweet from my earliest years, to become for me a subject of torture. Nor did the trial last merely for days or weeks: months have passed in this agony and I still await relief. I wish I could explain what I feel, but it is beyond my power. One must have passed through the tunnel to understand how black is its darkness; the fog that surrounds me finds its way into my very soul, and so blinds me that I can no longer see there the lovely picture of my promised home.... It has all faded away! When my heart, weary of the enveloping darkness, tries to find some rest and strength in the thought of a life to come, my anguish only increases. It seems to me that the darkness

itself, borrowing the voice of the unbeliever, cries mock-
ingly: "You dream of a land of light and fragrance, you
believe that the Creator of these wonders will be for ever
yours, you think one day to escape from the mists in which
you now languish. Hope on! Hope on! Look forward to
death! It will give you, not what you hope for, but a night
darker still, the night of utter nothingness!" This description of what I suffer, dear Mother, is as far removed from
reality as the painter's rough outline is from the model he
copies, but to write more might be to blaspheme...even
now I may have said too much. May God forgive me! He
knows how I try to live by faith, even though it affords me
no consolation. I have made more acts of faith during the
past year than in all the rest of my life.... Sometimes, I confess, a feeble ray of sunshine penetrates my dark night and
brings me a moment's relief, but after it has gone, the
remembrance of it, instead of consoling me, makes the
blackness seem deeper still. And yet I have never experienced more fully the sweetness and mercy of Our Lord.
He did not send this heavy cross when it would, I believe,
have discouraged me, but chose a time when I was able to
bear it. Now it does no more than deprive me of all natural satisfaction in my longing for heaven.[15]

This passage has been quoted in full because the Saint's own
words speak more directly to us than any commentary upon
them could ever do. They show us a childlike triumph of love
and faith in the midst of great suffering of both body and soul.
To St. Thérèse the first hæmorrhage is a message from the
Father calling his child to himself.

St. Thérèse's sickness made rapid progress, developing into
intestinal consumption of a very painful nature. Wasted with
fever as she was, and in continual darkness, the certainty that

[15] *Autobiography*, pp. 154–58.

her Father's love was always enveloping her, and that the divine will was tenderly working out its purpose in her, never left her. We find a quiet conviction in the reply she made on one occasion to Mother Agnes, who had remarked on the severity of her sufferings. "No," she said, "they are not terrible. How can a victim of love find anything terrible that is sent her by her Spouse? At each moment He sends me what I am able to bear—nothing more—and if He increases the pain, He increases also my strength to bear it." Then she added: "But I could never ask for greater sufferings—I am too little a soul; besides, being of my own choice, they would have to be borne by myself, and I have never been able to do anything when left to myself." [16]

If suffering could not cloud the certainty of her Father's love for her, still less did it quench her love for him; it did but serve to deepen and refine it. "Is it hard to suffer much?" she was asked. "No," she replied, "I am still able to tell God that I love Him and that is enough." [17] Later on she was at times unable even to do that. The infirmarian found her late one night with her hands joined and her eyes raised to heaven. "What are you doing?" she asked. "You ought to go to sleep." "I cannot, Sister", was the reply. "I am suffering too much, so I pray." "What do you say to Jesus?" "I say nothing; I just love Him." [18] At the last, unable to formulate any prayer at all, she says: "What is my spiritual life in sickness, you ask me. It is to suffer, and that is all." [19] St. Thérèse takes the only thing remaining, her suffering, and instead of saying that all spiritual life was made impossible by pain, she offers her pain to

[16] Ibid., pp. 233–34.
[17] *Novissima verba,* comp. by the Carmelites of Lisieux (Burns and Oates), p. 93.
[18] *Autobiography,* p. 237.
[19] *Novissima verba,* p. 108.

her Father in heaven as the greatest proof, the perfect expression of her love for him.

On the eve of his Passion Our Blessed Lord prayed that in the midst of their earthly sufferings his disciples should possess a joy and peace, supernatural, not of this world, which the world could neither give nor take away. It certainly was so with St. Thérèse. The doctor, after one of his visits, said to the Mother Prioress: "If you but knew what she is suffering! Never have I seen such suffering borne with such supernatural joy." [20] As we have already noted, she writes to her sister Céline: "I find only one joy, that of suffering, and this joy, which is not a pleasure of the senses, is above all joy." [21] Speaking of her great trial of faith, she says: "Notwithstanding this trial which deprives me of all feeling of joy, I can still say: *Thou hast given me, O Lord, a delight in thy doings*, for is there a greater joy than to suffer for Thy Love?" [22] Again, "Aridity increased, from neither heaven nor earth did I receive any consolation and yet in the midst of the waters of tribulation, I was the happiest of beings." [23]

Along with that supernatural joy went an equally supernatural peace, a peace which suffering, physical or spiritual, was utterly unable to touch. "Why are you so sad today, Mother?" she asked her sister who was praying by her sickbed. "Because you suffer so much", replied Mother Agnes. "Yes," said St. Thérèse, "but what peace as well! What peace!" [24] In the midst of her spiritual desolation, and ceaselessly assailed by temptations against faith, that peace prevailed. "My soul, notwithstanding the darkness, enjoys a most aston-

[20] *Autobiography*, p. 234.
[21] Ibid., p. 335.
[22] Ibid., p. 157.
[23] Ibid., p. 131.
[24] *Novissima verba*, p. 145.

ishing peace." [25] It was indeed *the peace of God, which surpasseth all understanding*,[26] given by Our Blessed Lord specially to those whom he draws closest to him through suffering—*peace through the blood of his cross*.[27] "The death of love that I desire is that of Jesus on the cross." [28] That desire, so long cherished by St. Thérèse, is now to become an accomplished fact, but to die thus did not mean to her to die in ecstasy. She is at pains to explain this to her sisters: "Do not be troubled if I suffer much and if you see in me, as I have already told you, no sign of happiness at the moment of my death.... Our Lord died a Victim of love indeed, and you know well how great was His agony." [29] And again: "Our Lord died on the cross in the midst of anguish, yet there, nevertheless, was the most glorious death of love that has ever been seen! To die of love is not to die in transports.... I tell you quite frankly that such, it seems to me, will be my experience." [30]

At the last, St. Thérèse's sufferings were intense. She became so weak that she could no longer make the slightest movement without help, the faintest sound in the sick-room was a source of acute distress, and she could get her breath only in gasps. Early in the morning of September 29, a rattle in the throat seemed to announce the end, but she lingered on during another night, the night of her deepest suffering and darkness. In the morning, casting a glance at the statue of the Blessed Virgin which was facing her bed, she said: "Oh, with what fervour I have prayed to her, but it was pure agony without any consolation. Earth's air is failing me, when shall

[25] Ibid., p. 128.
[26] Phil 4:7.
[27] Col 1:20.
[28] *Autobiography*, p. 240.
[29] *Novissima verba*, p. 21.
[30] Ibid., p. 37.

I breathe the air of heaven?"[31] All day the fever consumed her. "Ah," she said, "if this is the agony, what then is death?" Then, addressing the Prioress: "O Mother, I assure you that the chalice is full to the brim. My God, Thou art so good."[32] Then, in tones of deep conviction: "All that I have written of my desire for suffering is really true. I do not repent of having surrendered myself to love."[33] A little later she was heard to murmur: "I would never have believed it was possible to suffer so much, never! never! I can only explain it by my intense desire to save souls."[34]

At five o'clock Mother Agnes, who was alone with her, noticed a change. This time it was indeed the death agony. A hurried summons of the bell called the Community to the infirmary. For two hours the struggle continued, but towards seven o'clock, as the sufferer appeared to grow no worse, the Mother Prioress dismissed the Community. Looking towards her, St. Thérèse murmured: "Has the agony not come yet, Mother? Am I not going to die?" "Yes, my child, this is the agony, but God wishes perhaps to prolong it a few hours." "Very well then," she whispered, "let it be so. Oh, I would not wish to suffer less!" Then fixing her eyes on the crucifix she held in her hands, she murmured: "Oh, I love Him.... My God, I...love...Thee."[35] Those were her last words— an act of supernatural love, made utterly in the dark. Then suddenly, she, who for so long had been unable to move without the help of others, raised herself up and, opening her eyes, which shone with a joy which her sisters say no human words can describe, she fixed her gaze just above the statue of Our

[31] Ibid., p. 238.
[32] Ibid., p. 186.
[33] *Autobiography*, p. 239.
[34] *Novissima verba*, p. 189.
[35] *Autobiography*, pp. 239–40.

Lady. Remaining thus for the space of a *Credo*, she then surrendered her soul into her heavenly Father's arms, to the last his little child, the little victim of his Merciful Love.

Thus we see how faithfully St. Thérèse, in her Little Way, followed in the footsteps of Our Blessed Lord. Seeing everything *sub specie aeternitatis*, she, from her earliest days, knew that she came from God and went to God, that God was her Father and she his child, that heaven, not earth, was her home, yet that all that came to her in her life on earth lay within his infinite love and was ordered by his eternal will. So when suffering came, seeing it in that eternal setting, she was not dismayed nor did she regard herself as abandoned by her Father's love. So, as she goes to meet the suffering of her everyday life, a calm rhythm possesses her in all her ways. Suffering, so far from disposing her soul to despondency or despair, is seen to be the central secret of the spiritual life, the divine means of union between her soul and God, bring ing forth in its womb the first three fruits of the Spirit—love, joy, peace.

Just as Our Blessed Lord was conscious that he had a baptism wherewith he was to be baptized, and was straitened till it was accomplished, so too have we seen Thérèse pressing forward along the path of suffering till she dies a death of love like that of Jesus on the Cross. We have seen how tenderly her Father's love led her along the path of Spiritual Childhood to that long-desired consummation. Never was she more securely in her Father's arms than when, in utter darkness, she made her last act of supernatural love. But that is not the end. *I ascend to my Father and to your Father, to my God and to your God.*[36] In these words of Our Risen Lord the fullness of God's plan through suffering is revealed; and Christ crucified, so

[36] Jn 20:17.

baffling to merely human wisdom, is indeed seen to be both *the power of God and the wisdom of God.*[37]

Similarly, by the rapid ascent of Thérèse into heaven, and by the supernatural power and glory with which he has endowed her, God has given us in our own time a further and most vivid vindication of the fact that all the sufferings of this life lie within the hollow of his hand and that *to them that love God all things work together unto good.*[38] St. Thérèse has been given directly to us in our own day to lift our vision beyond this world and enable us to see our present sufferings in the light of the glory that is to come. *For which cause we faint not. . . . For that which is at present momentary and light of our tribulation worketh for us above measure exceedingly, an eternal weight of glory. While we look not at the things which are seen, but at the things which are not seen. For the things which are seen are temporal: but the things which are not seen are eternal.*[39]

---

[37] I Cor 1:24.
[38] Rom 8:28.
[39] 2 Cor 4:16–18.

XIV

SUFFERING (3)

WE HAVE SEEN, under the guidance of St. Thérèse, the place which suffering holds in the divine plan. It is the divinely appointed means, ordained from all eternity, whereby Almighty God, our heavenly Father, delivers us his children from our sin and selfishness, restores us, and reunites us with himself in supernatural love: so far from being something to be feared and dreaded, or even accepted merely with resignation, it is a treasure to be embraced with joy. We are now going to see how the loving acceptance of suffering not only reunites us ourselves with God, but is also the means by which we can help other souls.

The desire to offer herself for the salvation of souls came into the life of Thérèse at a very early age; it was towards the end of Mass in Lisieux when she was still only a girl of thirteen. She describes it thus:

One Sunday on closing my book at the end of Mass, a picture of the Crucifixion slipped partly out, showing one of the divine hands pierced and bleeding. An indescribable feeling, such as I had never before experienced, passed through me: my heart was torn with grief at the sight of the Precious Blood falling to the ground, with no one caring to treasure it as it fell. At once I resolved to remain continuously in spirit at the foot of the Cross, that I might

171

receive the divine dew of salvation and pour it forth upon souls. From that day the cry of my dying Saviour: "I thirst!" resounded incessantly in my heart, kindling within it new fires of zeal. To give my Beloved to drink was my constant desire; I was consumed with an insatiable thirst for souls, and I longed at any cost to snatch them from the everlasting flames of hell.[1]

This passage from the *Autobiography* is worth our most careful consideration. In those simple words, without involving us in the intricacies of theology, she takes us right to the source of the doctrine of vicarious suffering—the Cross. All flows from the Cross. It is at the foot of the Cross, therefore, that St. Thérèse will remain continuously in spirit, that she may receive the divine dew of salvation and pour it forth upon souls. This is the true order. The God-Man redeems us by his self-oblation consummated on Calvary. *By one oblation he hath perfected for ever them that are sanctified.*[2]

St. Thérèse saw quite clearly that the means, chosen from all eternity, whereby this should be accomplished was the loving acceptance of suffering by the beloved Son—a truth brought vividly home to her by the sight of the Sacred Hands pierced and bleeding, as the picture of the Crucifixion slipped from her missal at the end of Mass.

The vital principle of his self-oblation is his love for his Father expressed through a suffering obedience. That suffering obedience was consummated on the Cross. "Christ was made for us obedient unto death, even the death of the Cross."[3] To us, earthbound as we are, living in a world under the shadow of original sin, the word "obedience" carries with it a grim connotation; we shrink from it just because we know it means

[1] *Autobiography*, pp. 87–89.
[2] Heb 10:14.
[3] Divine Office for Holy Week.

suffering. Our Lord, on the contrary, embraced that obedience, and the suffering it involved, with eagerness. Wherein
lies the difference? In the two little words "for us". "Christ was
made for us obedient unto death." The key to Our Lord's loving acceptance of suffering lies in the fact that he saw it all in
the eternal plan of the Merciful Love for the souls of men. In
thus surrendering himself to his Passion, Our Lord offered himself as the Victim of his own Merciful Love for the souls of
men. In her contemplation of the Passion it was thus that St.
Thérèse always saw him. "Our Lord died upon the Cross the
most glorious death of love that has ever been seen." [4]

Hence flows redemption. *Being consummated, he became, to
all that obey him, the cause of eternal salvation.* [5] The moment of
the consummation of Our Lord's obedience, that is to say the
moment of his death—to human wisdom the grimmest
moment of the Passion—is seen to be precisely the moment
of the perfect revelation of the tenderness of the Merciful Love
of God, for by that death, and by that death alone, heaven is
once more opened to men. So the Church sings in her great
song of triumph: "Thou, having overcome the sting of death,
hast opened to believers the kingdom of heaven." But, in order
to enter thus into the kingdom of heaven, one condition is
absolutely necessary. *Omnibus obtemperantibus sibi*—to all that
obey him—what exactly does this mean? In the language of
St. Thérèse it means to all those who "remain continuously
in spirit at the foot of the Cross"; in other words, to all those
in whom there is the same mind *which was also in Christ Jesus,*
who was *obedient unto death, even to the death of the cross. For
which cause, God also hath exalted him and hath given him a name
which is above all names.* [6] Just as the loving acceptance of

[4] *Novissima verba*, comp. by the Carmelites of Lisieux (Burns and Oates), p. 37.
[5] Heb 5:9.
[6] Phil 2:5, 8–9.

suffering is the vital principle of Our Lord's self-oblation on the Cross, by which heaven was opened to all mankind, so the loving acceptance of suffering in union with the Cross was to be the vital principle of that self-oblation of St. Thérèse which should open the kingdom of heaven for her soul.

To offer him, and herself in him, that he might offer himself and suffer in her, and that so the whole redemptive activity of the Merciful Love on Calvary might be worked out in her own soul—that is what St. Thérèse means by offering herself as a little victim of the Merciful Love of God: little, because the more wholly she surrenders herself to the grace of her Baptism with the simple dependence of a little child, the more complete will be her offering, her conformity with Christ.

But it is not only for her own soul's sake that she will thus make her offering as she takes her stand at the foot of the Cross; she will offer herself also for the salvation of others. Our Lord has willed that we as members of his Mystical Body should make one thing, or, as St. Thomas says, "one mystical person" with him and, thus, should be able to appropriate the sacrificial activity of him who is our Head, so that he offers and suffers in us. It follows then that we appropriate that sacrificial activity in all the fulness of its application, not only for ourselves, but for all the members of the Mystical Body, and indeed for the whole human race, for God will have all men to be saved and to come to the knowledge of the truth. Thus it is that we are able to share by participation in Our Lord's redemptive work for the salvation of mankind. Thus Christ is fulfilled only through the sufferings of us, his members. *I ... fill up those things that are wanting of the sufferings of Christ, in my flesh, for his body, which is the church,*[7] says St. Paul.

---

[7] Col 1:24.

"I resolved to remain continuously in spirit at the foot of the
Cross, that I might receive the divine dew of salvation and
pour it forth upon souls", says St. Thérèse.

Christ can no longer suffer in his Natural Body; he does
so in his Mystical Body.

> The Church fills up those sufferings that are still lacking to
> the whole Christ; ... her passion is the extension of Christ's
> own passion and therefore an extension of his redemptive
> victory. By our willing acceptance of suffering, therefore,
> Christ continues to suffer in us and to work out to its com-
> pletion through the centuries the effect of his redemptive
> act for the salvation of the human race performed once for
> all on Calvary.[8]

Such is the theology of the profound doctrine of vicarious suffering underlying the simple language of the Little
Flower, when she says that she will remain continually in spirit
at the foot of the Cross in order to receive and pour forth the
divine dew of salvation upon souls. Thus it was not just a pious
picture which touched merely the imagination of St. Thérèse
at Mass that morning, but solid doctrine which illuminated
her soul by the light of the Holy Spirit.

Thus far we have considered the principles of the doctrine
of vicarious suffering in their relation to St. Thérèse and the
Little Way of Spiritual Childhood. We have seen how the
thirst for the salvation of souls first came into her life. We are
now to consider how that longing for the salvation of souls
found its practical expression in the everyday life in Carmel.
In a letter written shortly before her entry, we find that longing still uppermost in her mind. It is a remarkable passage
when we consider that she was only fourteen when she wrote

[8] Dom Bruno Webb, O.S.B., *Why Does God Permit Evil?* (Burns and Oates),
p. 87.

it. "It is such a joy", she says, "to think that for each pain cheerfully borne we shall love God more for ever. Happy should I be if at the hour of my death I could offer Jesus a single soul. There would be one soul less in hell, and one more to bless God for all eternity." [9] Once within Carmel, the salvation of souls through the loving acceptance of suffering becomes St. Thérèse's supreme preoccupation.

Suffering opened wide her arms to me from the first and I took her fondly to my heart. In the solemn examination before making the vows I then declared my reason for entering Carmel—"I have come to save souls and especially to pray for priests." The end cannot be reached without adopting the means, and since Our Lord had made me understand that it was through the Cross that He would give me souls, the more crosses I encountered the stronger became my attraction to suffering. [10]

The same theme runs through all her early letters written from the convent to her sister Céline: "Let us go forth to suffer together, dear sister, and let us offer our sufferings to Jesus for the salvation of souls." [11] Again: "Céline, during the fleeting moments that remain to us, let us save souls! I feel sure that our Spouse asks us for souls—above all for the souls of priests.... It is He who bids me tell you this. There is but one thing to do here below: to love Jesus and to save souls for Him that He may be more loved." [12] And what exactly are the sufferings that she will thus offer for the salvation of souls? We might expect that with a soul of such mettle as St. Thérèse's they would take the form of some elaborate or lofty penance. On the contrary, the sufferings that she offered were the every-

[9] *Autobiography*, p. 351.
[10] Ibid., p. 123.
[11] Ibid., p. 335.
[12] Ibid., p. 337.

day sufferings common to all of us—for example, daily worries or lack of courage.

> While in the world I used, on waking, to think of all the
> pleasant or unpleasant things which might happen throughout the day, and if I foresaw nothing but worries I got up
> with a heavy heart. Now it is the other way about. I think
> of the pains and of the sufferings awaiting me, and I rise,
> feeling all the more courageous in proportion to the opportunities I foresee of proving my love for Our Lord, and of
> gaining—mother of souls as I am—my children's livelihood.[13]

Speaking one day of lack of courage to a novice who was
wavering, she said:

> In being distressed at your lack of courage you are complaining at what ought to be your greatest happiness. If you
> fought only when you felt ready for the fray, where would
> be your merit? What does it matter even if you have no
> courage, provided you behave as though you were really
> brave? . . . Instead of grieving, be glad that, by allowing you
> to feel your own weakness, Our Lord is furnishing you with
> an occasion of saving a greater number of souls.[14]

St. Thérèse saw things in their totality. She saw the smallest detail of life as part of an infinite whole; she saw the smallest suffering in its direct relation to heaven.

What was it that enabled her to see things thus? It was her
littleness, that very thing in her which we so readily misunderstand. To the really little, to the really humble, to the soul,
that is to say, that is completely dependent upon God, the
whole universe and every detail of human life within it is a
unity. The smallest thing on earth is inseparably linked with

[13] Ibid., p. 308.
[14] Ibid., p. 309.

heaven. It is the humble who see things in their totality, because for them, God is the centre of everything. Their life therefore is a harmony, and they are at peace. On the other hand, the more grown-up we are, the more self-reliant and independent we become, the more is this truth hidden from our eyes, precisely because, self being the centre, we see things only after a fragmentary fashion. Life is full of discord and conflict; we become anxious and rebellious and know no peace.

We have seen that in the last years of her life St. Thérèse was overwhelmed with spiritual darkness and ceaselessly assailed by temptations against the faith, but so far from being dismayed or thinking, as we might so easily have done, that all was lost, she saw it all within the will of God. It was the fact that she was so completely her Father's little child which enabled her to see that this supreme trial against her faith was her supreme opportunity of securing the salvation of just those souls whom it is most difficult to save, the souls who have lost their faith. Such is St. Thérèse's thirst for souls that her very darkness becomes a prayer for unbelievers.

> Lord, Thy child believes firmly that Thou art the Light Divine; she asks pardon for her unbelieving brethren, and is willing to eat the bread of sorrow as long as Thou shalt will it so. For love of Thee she will sit at this table of bitterness where these poor sinners take their food, and will not rise from it till Thou givest the sign.... May all those upon whom faith does not shine at last see the light.... I tell Our Lord if He will deign to open it for eternity to poor unbelievers, I am content to sacrifice during my life all joyous thoughts of the home that awaits me.[15]

We might have expected that in her long and exhausting illness St. Thérèse's resolution might have been weakened by

[15] Ibid., pp. 156–57.

bodily weariness and her vision clouded by the nauseating details of the sick-room. On the contrary, every detail is pressed into the service of this ardent winner of souls. Almost the last thing she did before retiring finally to her sick-bed was to take a walk in the garden at the bidding of the infirmarian. Noticing how much the effort cost the invalid, a Sister said to her: "Sœur Thérèse, you would do much better to take a rest; walking can do you no good when you are suffering so much, you are only tiring yourself." "That is true," replied Thérèse, "but do you know what gives me strength? I offer each step for some missionary, thinking that somewhere far away, one of them is worn out by his apostolic labours, and to lessen his fatigue I offer mine to God." [16]

Confined within the limits of the infirmary, her vision as she lies upon her sick-bed becomes the more all-embracing. Every detail is gathered in, and nothing less than the whole Church is the object of her apostolic zeal. "I keep nothing in my hands", she says. "All that I have, all that I gain, that is for the Church and for souls." [17] And again: "I would not pick up a straw to avoid going to purgatory. All that I have done, I have done to give God pleasure and to save souls."[18] Six weeks before her death she said: "Do I wish to acquire merits? Yes indeed, but not for myself—for souls, for all the needs of the Church, in short, to scatter roses on the whole world, upon the just and upon sinners." [19]

Her field of activity is not limited to this world; in purgatory she would be active too. "If I go to purgatory I shall be quite contented, I shall do as did the three Hebrews. I shall walk in the midst of the furnace singing the song of

[16] Ibid., p. 215.
[17] *Novissima verba*, p. 57.
[18] Ibid., p. 93.
[19] Ibid., p. 137.

love. How happy I should be if, through that, I was able to deliver other souls and to suffer in their place, for then I should be doing good."[20] Should she go straight to heaven, well then, the attraction of heaven for her lies in the fact that there she will in the fullest measure be able to quench her thirst for God and for souls. "In heaven one sole expectation makes my heart beat fast. It is the love that I shall receive, and the love that I shall be able to give.... I think of all the good I shall do after my death.... I will help priests, missionaries, the whole Church."[21]

St. Thérèse never allowed her wide vision to dim the realization that, as she lay on her sick-bed, her power for saving souls lay in the offering of the pains of the present moment. In view of her extreme weakness the doctor ordered some strengthening remedies. She was distressed at first because of their cost. Afterwards she admitted: "I have made a covenant with God that they may be for the benefit of poor missionaries who have neither time nor means to take care of themselves."[22]

Not long before her death, she related to her sister an incident which perhaps more than any other shows the delicacy of her love for Our Lord, the intimacy of her conformity with him in his Passion, and the intensity of her love for souls.

On one occasion, during the "Great Silence", when I was in a high fever and parched with thirst, the infirmarian put a hot-water bottle to my feet and tincture of iodine on my chest. Whilst submitting to these remedies I could not help saying to Our Lord: "My Jesus, Thou seest I am already burning and they have brought me more heat and more fire. If instead they had given me even half a glass of water,

---

[20] Ibid., p. 48.
[21] Ibid., p. 61.
[22] *Autobiography*, p. 234.

what comfort it would have been! My Jesus! Thy child is very thirsty! She is glad however to have this opportunity of resembling Thee more closely and thus of saving souls." [23]

The material thus seized upon by St. Thérèse for the salvation of souls was something which may easily come the way of any of us—the unnecessary blunders of those who nurse us in our last sickness. No wonder that such fidelity roused the devil to fury. But all the spiritual suffering—and it was very great—with which he was allowed by Mighty God to afflict her during her last days on earth, was to St. Thérèse merely a further battle which she was waging for some other soul. One night she begged the Sister who was tending her to sprinkle holy water on the bed, saying:

The devil is near me: I do not see him but I feel his presence. He torments me; he holds me with a hand of iron, preventing me from getting the slightest relief; he increases my pain in order to lead me to despair.... And I cannot pray. All I can do is to look at the Blessed Virgin and say "Jesus". How necessary is that prayer at Compline: *Procul recedant somnia, et noctium phantasmata!* What I experience is altogether mysterious: I do not suffer for myself but for another soul...and the devil is angry.[24]

Till her very last moment upon earth St. Thérèse remained continually in spirit at the foot of the Cross, receiving the divine dew of salvation and pouring it forth upon souls. Thus did she fulfil to the uttermost the resolution which she had made years before, at the end of Mass, when she was only a girl of thirteen. The fruits of her loving acceptance of suffering as the divinely appointed means of saving souls became

[23] Ibid., p. 235.
[24] Ibid., p. 224.

increasingly evident every day. "If today the little Saint, as she is so often called, transforms countless hearts in such an amazing manner, if the good she does upon earth is beyond reckoning, we may believe without any doubt that she bought it all at the price with which Jesus bought back the souls of men—suffering and the Cross." [25] St. Thérèse's self-oblation still bears fruit in our own day; she has told us it will do so till the end of time.

> I will spend my heaven doing good upon earth. This is not impossible, for the angels keep watch over us while they enjoy the Beatific Vision. No, there cannot be any rest for me till the end of the world—till the angel shall have said: "Time is no more." Then shall I take my rest, then shall I be able to rejoice, because the number of the elect will be complete. [26]

[25] Ibid., p. 214.
[26] Ibid., p. 231.

XV

OUR LADY (1)

G OD HAS *predestinated us unto the adoption of children through
Jesus Christ,*[1] and in proportion as we realize that our
adopted sonship is our supreme glory and the foundation of
our hope, in that proportion shall we revere and love the
instrument ordained from all eternity through which the
design of Almighty God for our souls was to be accomplished—Mary. And what we shall value in Mary is that motherhood by which our adopted sonship came into being: *When
the fulness of the time was come; God sent his Son, made of a woman
... that we might receive the adoption of sons.*[2]

"The Blessed Virgin is more mother than queen." These
words contain the essence of St. Thérèse's devotion to Our
Lady, and that devotion is fully expressed in the conversation
with Mother Agnes in which they occur, a conversation which
took place only six weeks before Thérèse's death.

> One knows well that the Blessed Virgin is queen of
> heaven and earth, but she is more a mother than a queen,
> and I do not believe (as I have so often heard said) that
> because of her prerogative she will eclipse the glory of all
> the Saints, just as the sun when it rises blots out the light
> of the stars. That is indeed very strange! A mother who

[1] Eph 1:5.
[2] Gal 4:4–5.

could make the glory of her children disappear! I think just the opposite, and I believe that she will greatly increase the glory of the elect. It is well to speak of her prerogatives, but that is not enough. We must make her loved. If while listening to a sermon on the Blessed Virgin, one is constrained to exclaim to oneself from beginning to end: "Ah!... Ah!" one grows weary, and that does not lead on to love and imitation. Who knows if some soul might not go so far as to feel a certain estrangement from a creature that is so very much superior? The unique privilege of the Blessed Virgin is to have been exempt from original sin, and to be the Mother of God. And on this latter point Jesus has said to us: *Whosoever doeth the will of My Father in heaven, he is My brother, My sister and My mother.* On the other hand, we are happier than she is, for she has not the Blessed Virgin to love.... That is such an increase of joy for us, and a loss of joy for her! Oh, how I love the Blessed Virgin! [3]

In this passage the prerogatives of Mary are clear, and given their true place, but never are they allowed to cause any sense of separation and estrangement. Mary is the Mother of the Word made flesh, God Incarnate, but never is the divine Motherhood, with the splendours of its attendant prerogatives, allowed to obscure the equally vital truth that Mary is therefore the spiritual Mother of all the members of his Mystical Body: never is it allowed to obscure the truth that she who is the natural Mother of the *firstborn of many brethren* is the spiritual Mother of many children.

As, in our progress along the Little Way of Spiritual Childhood, we look upon Mary, our Mother, with the utter dependence of a little child—and precisely because we do so

---

[3] *Novissima verba,* comp. by the Carmelites of Lisieux (Burns and Oates), pp. 142–43.

regard her—our devotion will bear a double impress. Our littleness will light up and throw into brilliant relief the
magnificence of her splendour: we shall see her divine Maternity as something which indeed distinguishes her completely
from us—something unique, investing her with a glory far sur-
passing that of even the highest of the angels. At the same time,
our very littleness will enable us to realize that the glory which
distinguishes Our Lady from us is itself the bond which binds
us to her with an intimacy greater than any other known to
human kind—the intimacy of a mother with her little one.
To those who tread the Little Way, the glories of Mary are
indeed apparent, but they are all the time enveloped in her
Motherhood. The passage we have quoted is typical of this.
It opens with a clear statement of the glory of the divine
Maternity and closes on a note of intimacy possible only
between a very small child and its mother. "We are happier
than she is, for she has not the Blessed Virgin to love. . . . That
is such an increase of joy for us and a loss of joy for her! Oh,
how I love the Blessed Virgin!" That is a typically Thérèsian
intimacy, born, not of sentiment, but of her accurate grasp of
where Our Lady's greatness really lies—she is more Mother
than queen.

Since, then, the relationship of St. Thérèse to Our Lady is
essentially that of a little child to its mother, we find that relationship characterized throughout by the simplicity and
directness which belong so specially to little children.

> How very glad I should have been to be a priest [she said
> on one occasion], so as to preach about the Blessed Vir-
> gin! I feel that I should have needed to preach only once
> to make my thoughts understood. First I should have
> shown how little is known of the life of the Blessed Vir-
> gin. It is not well to say things about her that are unlikely,
> or that we do not know, as, for example, that at the age

of three she went to the Temple to offer herself to God with feelings of extraordinary fervour and on fire with love, while perhaps she went quite simply in obedience to her parents. Why, again, say, *à propos* of the prophetic words of the venerable Simeon, that the Blessed Virgin from that moment had constantly before her eyes the Passion of Jesus? *A sword of sorrow shall pierce thine own soul.* You see very well, my little Mother, that it was a prediction of what was to come later on. For a sermon on the Blessed Virgin to bear fruit it must manifest her real life such as the Gospel has set before us, and not her supposed life, and one can well understand that her real life at Nazareth and afterwards must have been quite ordinary. ... *He was subject to them.* How simple that is! Instead of showing the Blessed Virgin as all but inaccessible, one would show her as possible of imitation, practising the hidden virtues, and living by faith just as we do. And we should give proofs of this, taken from the Gospel, where we read: *They understood not the things which he said unto them.* And again: *His father and his mother were wondering at those things which were spoken concerning him.* That wonder implies a certain astonishment. Do you not find it so, Mother? . . .[4] How I love to sing to her:

> *Tu me le fais sentir, ce n'est pas impossible*
> *De marcher sur tes pas, ô Reine des élus!*
> *L'étroit chemin du ciel, tu l'as rendu visible*
> *En pratiquant toujours les plus humbles vertus.*[5]

St. Thérèse does indeed see Our Lady as the Mother of divine grace, as the instrument divinely chosen to give us the

---

[4] Ibid., pp. 149–52.

[5] "And thou, by practising the lowliest virtues here/ Hast shown us how to find and tread the narrow way./ O, Queen of the elect, if I but follow thee,/ Thou'lt guide my faltering feet so that they never stray."—"Pourquoi je t'aime, O Marie", *Poems*. Translated by D. A. P.

Sacred Humanity, the Word made flesh, the source from whom all grace flows; the Mother who, at Bethlehem, and supremely by her travail pangs on Calvary, brought her forth to supernatural life. But she does not halt here; she sees her above all as the Mother who, from moment to moment, watches over her with the most understanding and tender love, mothering her little one, and supplying her every need from the cradle to the grave. The consciousness of our need of this moment-to-moment mothering love of Mary will be in proportion to our littleness, for the truth that there is literally no grace which does not come to us through Mary is one which only the truly humble can realize and appropriate to themselves. Only the humble can realize the need of such a Mother, and out of their need they learn the intimate delicacy of their Mother's love, ever obtaining for them, by her all-powerful, unique, and universal supplication, just those graces which they need, not merely in the spiritual order but in the material order as well.

To that Mother's love, Thérèse responded with the spontaneity of a small child, looking to her for everything. On opening the *Autobiography*, we are met at once by an example of her trust in her heavenly Mother.

> When you, my Mother Prioress, asked me to write the story of my soul, I feared the task might unsettle me, but Our Lord has deigned to make me understand that by simple obedience I shall please Him best.... Before setting about my task, I knelt before the statue of Our Lady which has given us so many proofs of our heavenly Mother's loving care. As I knelt, I begged of that dear Mother to guide my hand, and so ensure that only what was pleasing to her should find place there.[6]

---

[6] *Autobiography*, p. 29.

Thus the *Autobiography* from which we are making our study comes in a real sense from Our Lady herself.

Little Thérèse was mothered, as indeed we all are, from the very font. On January 4, 1873, the day on which she was baptized in the church of Notre Dame at Alençon, Our Lady took her under her protecting care. When still only four years old, she used to be taken by her mother for country walks around Alençon. From these walks little Thérèse would return laden with bunches of wild flowers—daisies, buttercups, and wild poppies—which she had gathered here and there along the path. With these she would deck the statue of Our Lady which stood in the home of the Martin family in the Rue de Blaise, which later on was to play so great a part in the life of the Little Flower. Even at that early age, Thérèse seems to have had some understanding of the offering of flowers as the symbol of the oblation of her life: at all events her devotion to Our Lady was very real.

> It is quite a ceremony [writes Marie to Pauline], this preparation for the month of Mary. Mamma is so very particular about it, more particular than the Blessed Virgin herself. She wants hawthorn branches reaching to the ceiling, the walls decorated with evergreens, etc. Thérèse is in wonderment at it all. Every morning she goes running with delight to say her prayers there.[7]

On August 28, 1879, Madame Martin died, when Thérèse was four and a half years old. With the loss of her earthly mother, she turned more than ever to her Mother in heaven. In the first year at Les Buissonnets at Lisieux, the little child of five was considered too young to be present every evening at the May devotions. It made no difference. She had a chest

---

[7] August Pierre Laveille, *St. Thérèse de l'Enfant Jésus* (Clonmore and Reynolds), p. 58.

of drawers in her elder sister's room converted into a Madonna altar, with tiny flower-vases and candlesticks. Victoire, the devoted servant, alone formed the congregation at these ceremonies, of which the principal exercise was the recitation of the *Memorare*.

The first years at Les Buissonnets, though quiet and peaceful, were not easy for Thérèse. As we have already seen, it was during this time that Pauline left home to enter Carmel. That separation, coming so soon after her mother's death, was more than Thérèse's sensitive nature could stand: she became desperately ill. But the Mother of Sorrows, who herself became the Mother of the Man of Sorrows in order that the world might be rescued from its suffering, is truly the Mother of Consolation, ever at hand with her perpetual succour to mother her children in their pain. We will let St. Thérèse herself describe what happened.

> I became so ill that, humanly speaking, there was no hope of recovery. I do not know how to describe this extraordinary illness. I said things which I did not think, and I did things as though I were forced to do them in spite of myself. Most of the time I appeared delirious, and yet I am quite certain that I was never for one moment deprived of my reason.... What fears the devil inspired. Everything frightened me.... In the hours when the pain was less acute, it was my delight to weave garlands of daisies and forget-me-nots for Our Lady's statue. We were then in the lovely month of May, and the earth was adorned with the flowers of spring. Only the Little Flower drooped and seemed to have faded for ever. But close beside her was a radiant Sun, the miraculous statue of the queen of Heaven, and towards that glorious Sun the Little Flower would often turn. Father came into my room one morning, evidently in the greatest distress. Going up to Marie, he gave her some gold pieces, and

bade her write to Paris for a novena of Masses to be said at the shrine of Our Lady of Victories to obtain the cure of his little queen. His faith and love touched me very deeply and I longed to get up and tell him I was cured. Alas! my wishes would not work a miracle, and an extraordinary miracle was necessary if I were to be restored to health. But it was wrought and my recovery made complete by the intercession of Our Lady of Victories.... One Sunday during the novena, all efforts having failed, Marie was kneeling in tears at the foot of my bed. Then, looking towards the statue, she implored Our Lady's assistance with all the fervour of a mother who begs the life of her child and will not be refused. Léonie and Céline joined in her prayer, and that cry of faith forced the gates of heaven. Utterly exhausted and finding no help on earth, I too sought my heavenly Mother's aid, and entreated her with all my heart to have pity on me. Suddenly the statue became animated and radiantly beautiful—with a divine beauty that no words of mine can ever convey. The look upon Our Lady's face was unspeakably kind and sweet and compassionate, but what penetrated to the very depths of my soul was her gracious smile. Instantly all my pain vanished; silently my tears began to fall, tears of purest joy. "Our Blessed Lady has come to me, she has smiled on me! How happy I feel! But I shall tell no one, for if I do my happiness will leave me!..." From that moment Our Lady's Flower gathered such strength that five years later she unfolded her petals on the fertile mountain of Carmel.[8]

During those five years St. Thérèse was to meet with many difficulties and temptations, but before they befell her she had the great joy of making her First Communion. In the afternoon she was chosen to make the Act of Consecration to Our

[8] *Autobiography*, pp. 63–67.

Lady on behalf of all the first communicants, and in her
description of this we see how closely she was united with her
heavenly Mother on that happy day.

> In the afternoon [she writes], I read the Act of Consecra-
> tion to Our Lady in the name of all the first communicants;
> probably the choice fell on me because my own earthly
> mother had been taken from me while I was still so young.
> I put my whole heart into the reading of the prayer and
> besought Our Lady always to watch over me. It seemed to
> me that she looked down lovingly and once more smiled
> on her Little Flower. I recalled the visible smile which had
> cured me, and my heart was full of all I now owed her, for
> it was no other than she who, on that very May morning,
> had placed in the garden of my soul her Son Jesus—*the*
> *Flower of the field and the Lily of the valleys.*[9]

Our Lady is the Mediatrix of all Graces, an office which
implies the most intimate relationship with every one of her
children; in the passage just quoted, St. Thérèse expresses this
truth in a way which everyone can understand.

She was by now growing up into a beautiful and attractive
girl: this was to be the cause of temptation to her more than
once. In order to complete her education, her father sent her
to have private lessons with a lady who, in addition to being
a competent teacher, was evidently a centre of society in
Lisieux.

> Visitors [writes St. Thérèse] were often shown into the
> quaintly furnished room where I sat surrounded by my
> books; though seemingly absorbed in my work, little
> escaped my attention, even of what it would have been far
> better for me not to hear. One visitor remarked on my
> beautiful hair; another enquired, as she left the room, who

[9] Ibid., p. 75.

was the pretty little girl. Such remarks, all the more flattering because I was not meant to hear them, left a feeling of pleasure, clearly proving that I was full of self-love: had not my heart been lifted up to God from its first awakening, had the world smiled on me from the cradle, there is no knowing what I might have become.[10]

Instinctively she turns to her heavenly Mother. "I resolved", she says, "to consecrate myself in a special way to Our Lady, and therefore I sought admission into the Sodality of the Children of Mary." [11]

St. Thérèse was soon to realize the need of Our Lady's protection, for temptation was to come to her in a more subtle form. Her father had planned that she should go with him on a visit to Rome: in order to do this they joined the diocesan pilgrimage from Bayeux. It was arranged that the projected journey should be not only an act of filial loyalty to the Holy Father, but at the same time a pleasure trip. The programme was made so attractive that many of the leading families in Lisieux decided to take part. Instinctively Thérèse realized the danger. On passing through Paris, she was able to fulfill one of her greatest desires: she was able to visit the shrine of Our Lady of Victories. The fact that her miraculous cure had been made public had caused her great suffering. Her visit to Our Lady of Victories set this at rest.

> I can never tell you [she says] what I felt at her shrine; the graces she granted me there were like those of my First Communion Day, and I was filled with happiness and peace. In this holy spot the Blessed Virgin, my Mother, told me plainly it was really she who had smiled on me and cured me. With intense fervour I entreated her to guide me always, to realize my heart's desire by sheltering me

[10] Ibid., p. 81.
[11] Ibid., p. 82.

under her spotless mantle, and to remove from me every occasion of sin. I was well aware that during the pilgrimage I should come across things that might disturb me. . . .[12]

She was right. A young man, one of the pilgrims, was greatly attracted by her and showed her marked attention. She received his advances with reserve, and as soon as she was alone with Céline she confided her trouble. "Oh, it is indeed time that Jesus took me away from the world. I feel that my heart would easily let itself be taken captive by affection, and where others have perished I would perish too, for every creature is weak, myself in particular."[13]

We have seen then that, through becoming the little children of our Father in heaven, we have Mary for our Mother. We have also seen that her Motherhood does not cease there, but that she continues from moment to moment to watch over us with the tenderest care. All this we have found exemplified in the life of St. Thérèse. Conscious of her Mother's love enveloping her from the very first, she responds to that love with all the surrender of a very little child—in her early days at Alençon, in her great sorrow at her mother's death, throughout her schooldays, and during the struggles she endured in following her vocation. In our next chapter we hope to show how the interplay of Our Lady's motherly care on the one side, and St. Thérèse's trustful and childlike response on the other, grows and deepens throughout her life in Carmel, throughout her last sickness, and, above all, in the hour of her death, when a little one most needs its mother's care.

[12] Ibid., p. 104.
[13] Laveille, *St. Thérèse*, p. 293.

XVI

OUR LADY (2)

WE HAVE CONSIDERED so far the part played by Our Lady in St. Thérèse's life up to the time of her entry into Carmel; within Carmel's walls we find her intimacy with Our Lady developed in the endless everyday trials and disappointments of her convent life, just such trials and disappointments as have their obvious parallels in our own life. Once again she is a model and guide whom we can all follow.

One such disappointment came to her towards the end of her novitiate; her profession was postponed for eight months, and she describes this delay as follows:

At the close of my year of novitiate, Mother Marie Gonzague told me I must not think of profession, as the Superior of the Carmel had expressly forbidden it, and I must wait for eight months more. Though at first I found great difficulty in being resigned to such a sacrifice, divine light soon penetrated my soul. ... Since I belonged to Our Lord and was His little plaything to amuse and console Him, it was for me to do His Will and not for Him to do mine. I understood also that on her wedding-day a bride would be scarcely pleasing to the bridegroom if she were not arrayed in magnificent attire. Now, I had not as yet laboured with that end in view. Turning therefore to Our Lord, I said to Him: "I do not ask Thee to hasten the day of my profession; I will wait as long as it may please Thee, but I can-

not bear that my union with Thee should be delayed through any fault of mine. I will set to work and prepare a wedding-dress adorned with all kinds of precious stones."
... Our Lady helped me with my wedding-dress, and no sooner was it completed than all obstacles vanished and my profession was fixed for September 8th.[1]

As a result of the delay, the date actually chosen for St. Thérèse's profession was Our Lady's birthday. Thus the delay, which at first seemed such an unrelieved disappointment, was the very means of uniting her in a special way to the Mother who had prepared her soul for the great event.

When at the close of that glorious day [writes St. Thérèse], I laid my crown of roses as was usual at Our Lady's feet, it was without regret: I felt that time could never take away my happiness. Was not the Nativity of Mary a beautiful feast on which to become the spouse of Christ? It was the little newborn Mary who presented her Little Flower to the little Jesus. That day everything was little except the graces I received, except my peace and joy as I gazed, when night came down, upon the glorious star-lit sky, and thought that before long I should take flight to heaven, and there be united to my Spouse in eternal bliss.[2]

We must be careful not to miss the point in this passage. It does not lie in the Saint's appreciation of the star-lit sky as a symbol of eternal life, but in the words: "It was the little new-born Mary who presented her Little Flower to the little Jesus." Why does St. Thérèse, at that supreme moment of her vocation, the very day of her profession, linger thus upon the thought of her littleness? Is she just a sheltered nun, altogether lacking in any understanding of the ruthless realities of human life, playing with pious fancies while the world outside suffers

[1] *Autobiography*, pp. 131–33.
[2] Ibid., p. 136.

and dies? It is not so: never once is St. Thérèse divorced from reality, least of all on the day of her profession. On the contrary, she is in perfect harmony with Holy Scriptures. It was out of her littleness—*He hath regarded the humility of His handmaid*—that Mary made her complete offering of herself; her *fiat mihi secundum verbum tuum,* and the Incarnation and the whole of our Redemption was set in motion. It was out of his "littleness", his complete dependence upon his Father's will—*he humbled himself, becoming obedient unto death*[3]—that Our Lord made his perfect offering of himself upon the Cross, and the whole world was saved. Next to her heart, on this the day of her profession, St. Thérèse bore a slip of paper on which she had written: "I offer myself to Thee, O my Beloved, that Thou mayest ever perfectly accomplish Thy Holy Will in me"[4] It was precisely out of her littleness that St. Thérèse was able to make the offering with such perfection that today the whole Church resounds with her glory Thus, on littleness in union with Jesus and Mary, did little Thérèse, on the day of her profession, lay the foundation of her Little Way of Spiritual Childhood.

One of the things which cause us most distress as we try to follow the Little Way of St. Thérèse is the complete absence of any consolation and the sense of utter weariness which so often attends us during our prayers. We all suffer from this: it is when it occurs at Mass that it is most disconcerting. If, so we argue, the stream of grace is shut off at the very source, how can there be any progress in our spiritual life? We grow disheartened, and our fervour begins to fail. In our innate self-reliance, we fuss and fret and either turn in upon ourselves to examine our consciences afresh—with the only result that we become still more discouraged—or else we turn outwards to

[3] Phil 2:8.
[4] *Autobiography*, p. 136.

new and varied prayers and devotions which equally fail to lead us anywhere. We will so insist on trying to make earth reach to heaven. Now, part of St. Thérèse's great appeal is the fact that she experienced that lack of any consolation, that utter weariness, for the greater part of her life, especially in connection with her Mass and her Communion: it is no less part of her appeal that she shows us the way in which to meet it. Instead of being self-reliant, and fussing and fretting as we do, she, realizing her littleness and her utter dependence, remains calm and undisturbed, and instead of trying to make earth reach heaven, she calls heaven down to earth to work out in her soul what she cannot achieve for herself: and as she is a simple child of Mary, it is her Mother in heaven whom she calls down to her aid.

> There is no time [she writes] when I have less consolation than in my thanksgivings after Communion—yet this is not to be wondered at since it is not for my own satisfaction that I desire to receive Our Lord, but solely to give Him pleasure. Picturing my soul as a piece of waste ground, I beg of Our Lady to take away my imperfections which are as heaps of rubbish, and beautify it with her own adornments.... It seems to me that Jesus is well pleased to find Himself welcomed with such magnificence, while I too share His joy. But this does not keep off distractions and drowsiness, and I often resolve to continue my thanksgiving throughout the day for having made it so badly in choir.[5]

St. Thérèse's way of dealing with the situation is fundamental. She takes those human feelings which seem to us to indicate the loss of supernatural grace and the closing to us of the gates of heaven and makes them the very means of a closer

[5] Ibid., p. 142.

intimacy with Our Lord and his Blessed Mother and of a fuller
inflowing of the life of supernatural grace into her soul: and
it is precisely the realization of her littleness that makes this
possible. Mary is her spiritual Mother: she, Thérèse, is her
child born of that Mother's travail-pangs at the foot of Calvary. She even tells Our Blessed Lady that Our Lord, when
he comes to her heart in her Communion, thinks that it is
within his holy Mother he comes again to rest.

> *Et je suis ton enfant, O ma Mère chérie!*
> *Tes vertus, ton amour ne sont-ils pas à moi?*
> *Aussi, lorsqu'en mon cœur descend la blanche Hostie,*
> *Jésus, ton doux Agneau, croit reposer en toi!* [6]

Her certainty of her heavenly Mother's help did not
depend upon any consciousness of that Mother's presence, or
of her action upon her soul, for, as she tells us, the distraction
and drowsiness continued. It depended upon a loving trust,
born of faith in the full Catholic doctrine of the Motherhood
of Mary—a simple faith which does not belong to the wise
and prudent, but is given to little ones.

If we are discouraged by difficulties at prayer, we are often
far more discouraged by the apparently endless activities of our
daily routine. Now the difficulty of all routine is that it seems
to stretch far ahead into the future without any relief, and so
easily becomes monotonous and wearying. How does St.
Thérèse meet the difficulty? Well, little children do not worry
about the future, so she meets it with the surrender of a little
child. "If I did not simply live from one moment to another,
it would be impossible for me to be patient, but I look only

---

[6] "Since thou to me, thy child, beloved Mother art,/ Thy virtues and thy love,
are they not wholly mine?/ So when the frail white Host descends into my
heart,/ Jesus, thy tender Lamb, thinks to find rest in thine."—"Pourquoi je
t'aime, O Marie", *Poems*. Translated by D. A. P.

at the present. I forget the past, and take good care not to forestall the future. When we yield to discouragement or despair,
it is usually because we think too much about the past or the
future."[7] And in this surrender it is to her Mother Mary that
she commits herself for protection and for guidance.

> O Vierge Immaculée! O toi, la douce Etoile.
> Qui rayonne Jésus et qui m'unit à Lui,
> O mère! laisse-moi me cacher sous ton voile,
> Rien que pour aujourd'hui.[8]

Many of us have the responsibility of educating, or in some
way of guiding, others. St. Thérèse offers us invaluable advice
in this matter—the fruit of her experience in guiding the
novices entrusted to her care. Conscious from the first of her
inability to shoulder the responsibilities which the task
involved, she turned in complete dependence to Our Lord and
his holy Mother.

> I saw at a glance that the task was beyond my strength, and
> quickly taking refuge in Our Lord's arms, I imitated those
> babes who, when frightened, hide their faces on their
> father's shoulder. "Thou seest, Lord," I cried, "that I am
> too little to feed Thy little ones, but if, through me, Thou
> wilt give to each what is suitable, then fill my hands, and,
> without quitting the shelter of Thy arms, or even turning
> my head, I will distribute Thy treasures to the souls who
> come to me for food."[9]

To the novices expressing their surprise at the unfailing wisdom with which she met their needs, she replied: "This is my

---

[7] *Autobiography*, p. 222.

[8] "Thy light, O purest Virgin, Star serene,/ Draws me to Jesus by His own
bright ray./ Hide me, my Mother. Be thy veil my screen,/ For this one day."—
"Mon chant d'aujourd'hui", *Poems*. Translated by D. A. P.

[9] *Autobiography*, p. 175.

secret: I never reprimand you without first invoking Our
Blessed Lady, asking her to inspire me with whatever will be
for your greatest good. Often I am myself astonished at what
I say, but as I say it I feel I make no mistake, and that it is Jesus
who speaks by my lips." [10]

By her complete dependence on Jesus and Mary, St.
Thérèse was established in that supernatural detachment
which is vital if, in our dealing with others, we are to guide
them according to the will of God, and not according to
human feeling, to mere human sentiment. The most difficult
thing, St. Thérèse tells us, is to point out the will of God when
it is painful to the human nature of the person it is our duty
to guide. Upon our fidelity at such times all may depend. On
one occasion St. Thérèse had had to treat a novice with severity and, afterwards, was greatly tempted to go back on what
she had said.

> Only too happy [she writes] to follow the dictates of my
> heart, I hastened to serve some food less bitter to the taste.
> But I soon discovered that I must not go too far, lest a sin-
> gle word should bring to the ground the edifice that had
> cost so many tears. If I let fall the slightest remark that might
> seem to soften the hard truths of the previous day, I noticed
> my little Sister trying to take advantage of the opening thus
> afforded. Then I had recourse to prayer, I turned to Our
> Blessed Lady, and Jesus was victorious. [11]

For St. Thérèse, in her Little Way with others as in the Little
Way of her own spiritual life, it was always *per Mariam ad Jesum*.

So in the last illness of St. Thérèse, there is, in the midst
of the most acute suffering, an ever increasing interplay of care
and confidence between the Mother of Sorrows and her
suffering child.

[10] Ibid., p. 230.
[11] Ibid., p. 178.

As we come to those final months of St. Thérèse's life on earth—months so vital to her apostolate both then and since—it would seem best to retell the story, already told in chapter 3, emphasizing this time how at each turn she sought her heavenly Mother's aid and counsel.

On July 8, 1897, St. Thérèse became so ill that it was necessary to move her into the infirmary. As she was led from her cell, she said: "I have suffered greatly here. I would have liked to die here." On a table near her bed, her sister had placed the miraculous statue of the Blessed Virgin which had once cured her. On entering the infirmary, St. Thérèse paused and gazed upon it. "Never has it appeared so beautiful to me", she said to her sister Marie, who, before, had witnessed her cure, "but today it is the statue; before, as you well know, it was not the statue." [12]

During the Saint's last four months on earth, the thought of Our Blessed Mother seems never to have been absent from her mind. Knowing that her sufferings were causing pain to those around her, she said:

> I have asked the Blessed Virgin not to let me be as exhausted as I have been these last few days. I know very well that I have distressed you. Today she has heard me. O my little sister, I am so happy. I see that I am going to die soon, I am sure of it. I should like to have a beautiful death just to give you pleasure. I have asked it of the Blessed Virgin. To ask it of the Blessed Virgin is not the same thing as to ask it of God. She knows well what to do with my little wishes. She will decide whether to ask for them or not.... After all, it is for her to decide so as not to force God to hear me, but to leave all to His will. [13]

[12] August Pierre Laveille, *St. Thérèse de l'Enfant Jésus* (Clonmore and Reynolds), p. 359.

[13] *Novissima verba*, comp. by the Carmelites of Lisieux (Burns and Oates), p. 19.

Thérèse showed the same reliance on Our Lady's all-powerful supplication when a little later on she said: "I very often ask the Blessed Virgin to tell God that He must not bother Himself on my account, and that she will look after my commissions."[14] Recording in the *Autobiography* the interview with her father, in which she first told him of her desire to enter Carmel, she had written:

> Father, plucking a little white flower growing on a low stone wall, gave it to me and remarked with what loving care God had brought it to bloom, and preserved it until that day. I thought I was listening to my own life-story, so close was the resemblance between the little flower and little Thérèse.... I fastened my little flower to a picture of Our Lady of Victories, so that the Blessed Virgin smiles upon it, and the Infant Jesus seems to hold it in His hand. It is there still, but the stalk is now broken close to the root. No doubt God wishes me to understand that He will soon sever all the earthly ties of His Little Flower, and will not leave her to fade here below.[15]

On one occasion when she had been badly misunderstood, she said nothing at the time, but afterwards, to someone who had noticed it, she said: "The Blessed Virgin kept everything in her heart. They cannot blame me for doing what she did."[16]

On July 25, Mother Agnes remarked that death was very distressing to those who had to look upon it. At once Thérèse's thoughts turned to her heavenly Mother in her hour of dereliction. "The Blessed Virgin", she replied, "held the dead body of her Son in her arms, disfigured and bloodstained. At least you will not see me like that. Ah! I do not know how

[14] Ibid., p. 28.
[15] *Autobiography*, p. 95.
[16] *Novissima verba*, p. 46.

she did it. I wonder if they brought me to you in that state what you would do." [17] When one of her sisters expressed the fear that she would die during the night, she replied: "I shall not die during the night. I have had the wish not to die during the night, and I have asked that of the Blessed Virgin." [18] As August wore on, St. Thérèse seemed overwhelmed with suffering, both spiritual and physical, for, as we have seen, in addition to her bodily pain, she was afflicted with spiritual desolation and with temptations against the faith, which were ceaseless. On August 10, she made allusion to those interior sufferings. Mother Agnes was talking with her about heaven, Our Saviour, and the Blessed Virgin. Involuntarily St. Thérèse let a deep sigh escape her. Her sister said: "That sigh tells me how much you are suffering interiorly." Fearing lest she might have betrayed some lack of trust in her heavenly Mother's care, Thérèse immediately replied: "Yes! but ought one, loving God and the Blessed Virgin so much, to have those thoughts?... At least I do not dwell on them." [19]

Her physical weakness became extreme. A week later, August 19, she made the last Communion of her life. Her preparation for that last Communion was a night of unrelieved pain. In consequence of her extreme weakness she nearly fainted while listening, before Holy Communion, to the chanting of the *Miserere*, even though it was chanted in subdued tones. Afterwards she said: "Oh! if you only know what this trial is like! Last night, being unable to do more, I asked the Blessed Virgin to take my head in her hands so that I might be able to bear it." [20] At times she was unable to pray at all; still she was undefeated. "I cannot pray, I can only look at the

[17] Ibid., p. 85.
[18] Ibid., p. 91.
[19] Ibid., p. 130.
[20] Ibid., p. 138.

Blessed Virgin, and say: 'Jesus'."[21] To the infirmarian, St. Thérèse said: "Pray much to the Blessed Virgin for me, for if you were sick I should pray much for you. When it is for oneself, one is not very bold."[22] Then she added: "When we pray to the Blessed Virgin and she does not hear us, we ought to leave her to do what she pleases without insisting, and not to go on tormenting ourselves any more."[23]

During all her intense suffering, St. Thérèse was continually thinking of others. Sister Geneviève of the Holy Face— "little Céline, sweet companion of my childhood", as St. Thérèse used to call her—slept in a cell close to the infirmary so as to be ready at hand. "I asked the Blessed Virgin last evening", Thérèse told a Sister, "that I might not cough during the night so that Sister Geneviève might be able to sleep, but I added: 'If you do not do this for me, I shall love you all the more.'"[24] She had always dreaded a long illness which might make her a burden to the Community. Looking at the statue of Our Lady, the statue which had given her so many evidences of her heavenly Mother's tender care, she said: "My Mother, what makes me want to go is that I cause so much fatigue to the infirmarian, and such grief to my little sisters to see me suffering so much. Oh, I should indeed be glad to go."[25]

On September 11 she rallied a little, and her sisters tell how very feebly she set to work to make two little crowns of wild flowers for the statue of Our Lady. One was placed at Our Lady's feet, the other in her hands. The Sister sitting with her, pointing to the latter, said: "Perhaps this is destined for you." Thérèse replied: "Oh no! the Blessed Virgin can do what she

[21] Laveille, *St. Thérèse*, p. 367.
[22] *Novissima verba*, p. 148.
[23] Ibid., p. 154.
[24] Ibid., p. 135.
[25] Ibid., p. 161.

likes with it. I give it to her for her pleasure." [26] The significance of such an incident is all the more compelling when we realize that St. Thérèse had no special sense of Our Lady's presence with her: still less did she ever see her. That was exactly what the little Saint preferred. "I love the Blessed Virgin and the Saints very much, and yet I do not desire to see them. I prefer to live by faith." [27] The whole of St. Thérèse's last illness was passed in the obscurity of faith, and in that obscurity of faith it was to Our Lady that she continually turned. At half-past two on September 30, the day of her death, she raised herself in bed, which she had been unable to do for weeks, exclaiming: "My God, whatsoever Thou wilt, but have pity on me. Sweet Virgin Mary, come to my aid." [28] Towards three o'clock the Mother Prioress placed a picture of Our Lady of Mount Carmel upon her knees. Looking at it for a moment, she said: "O Mother, present me very soon to the Blessed Virgin. Prepare me to die well." [29] At six o'clock, as the convent bells rang the evening Angelus, she gazed appealingly at the statue of the Blessed Virgin. Was she remembering the last poem she wrote?

> *Toi qui vins me sourire au matin de ma vie,*
> *Viens me sourire encore. Mère, voici le soir.*[30]

After one more hour of intense suffering she gave up her soul to Almighty God, to the end a true child of her heavenly Father and a true child of Mary.

[26] Ibid., p. 171.
[27] Ibid.
[28] Ibid., p. 187.
[29] Ibid., p. 239.
[30] "Mother, whose smile consoled me in the dawn,/ Smile on me once again, for darkness falls."—"Pourquoi je t'aime, O Marie", *Poems*. Translated by D. A. P.

XVII

THE SHOWER OF ROSES

A FTER MY DEATH I will send down a shower of roses."[1] Of all the prophecies made by St. Thérèse during her last illness, this is the most widely known. It has taken hold of the public imagination, and the favours she confers on those who invoke her are spoken of as roses throughout the whole Catholic world.

Some there are, however, who frankly regret this and do not hesitate to say so. Some of them have never come into close contact with the Saint precisely because of the "rose business". Others have a real devotion to St. Thérèse and clearly understand her message, yet they find the rose *motif* a stumbling block. They realize that she made the prophecy, that she has fulfilled it and has indeed showered roses upon the earth, but they regret that so much has been made of this particular saying.

It is our purpose in this final chapter to show that there is nothing sentimental in the imagery of the rose: that so far from being the exaggeration of an aspect of St. Thérèse's message, it is inseparable from the reality it is meant to convey and is an integral part of her mission: that the Holy See has set its seal to it, and that, through this symbol, the Saint has, in the

[1] *Autobiography*, p. 230.

providence of God, brought home to ordinary men and women some of the sternest and most profound lessons of the spiritual life.

In the natural order Almighty God gives us the rose, the most beautiful of flowers, in a setting of thorns, and those who want to pick it know that they may get hurt. Similarly, in the supernatural order, in the Catholic Church, the rose is inseparably linked with sacrifice and suffering, for in Catholic tradition the rose is the flower of martyrdom. In the Papal Brief read in St. Peter's during the ceremony of St. Thérèse's Beatification, the Holy See uses this very phrase: "In the Catholic Church the white lilies of the virgins are intertwined with the red roses of martyrdom, that splendid crown which adorns the Immaculate Bride of Christ." [2] In speaking thus, the Holy See is using the traditional language of the Church from as far back as the third century, for it is to be found in the writings of St. Cyprian.

> O blessed Church of ours.... She was white before in the works of the brethren, now she is become purple in the blood of martyrs. Among her flowers are wanting neither lilies nor roses. Now let each strive for the highest dignity of either honour. Let them receive crowns either white as of labours, or purple as of suffering. In the heavenly camp both peace and strife have their own flowers with which the soldier of Christ may be crowned for glory.[3]

Five centuries later this passage of St. Cyprian is echoed almost word for word by our own countryman, the Venerable Bede, and finds its place in the Divine Office for the feast of All Saints. We find the same connexion between the rose and martyrdom in the hymn for Lauds of the feast of the Holy Innocents:

[2] *The Story of the Canonization* (Burns and Oates), p. 96.
[3] St. Cyprian, Epist. 10: *To the Martyrs (ad fin.)*.

Salvete, flores Martyrum,
Quos lucis ipso in limine
Christi insecutor sustulit,
Ceu turbo nascentes rosas.[4]

Finally, in the more modern office of Our Lady of Sorrows, the same language is addressed to Our Blessed Lady herself:

Ave, princeps generosa
Martyrumque prima rosa.

Since the rose is regarded by the Church as the flower of martyrdom, we should expect her child, little Thérèse, to see it in the same way.

The image of the shower of roses is inseparable from the truth it foretold; it was regarded by St. Thérèse as a part of her mission. During her last illness she refers to it again and again. The prophecy, "After my death I will send down a shower of roses", does not stand alone, for a few days later she said: "I will spend my heaven doing good upon earth."[5] She then proceeds to tell us exactly what form this good will take. "When I have gone to heaven you must often, with your little sacrifices and prayers, give me the pleasure of showering a rain of graces upon souls."[6] "In heaven I shall obtain abundance of graces for those who have done me good."[7] As Thérèse lies waiting for death, she looks forward to the fulfilment of her prophecy. "I should not be happy in heaven if I were not able to provide little pleasures on earth for those

[4] "All Hail! ye infant martyr flowers/ Cut off in life's first dawning hours,/ As rosebuds snapped in tempest strife,/ When Herod sought your Saviour's life." (Dr. Neale's translation.)

[5] *Novissima verba*, comp. by the Carmelites of Lisieux (Burns and Oates), p. 75.

[6] Ibid., p. 162.

[7] Ibid., p. 47.

I love." [8] "God would not have given me the desire to do good upon earth after my death if He did not will to realize it." [9] Not only will she send down from heaven a shower of roses, she herself "will come down".[10] "Later on I shall be standing beside the little baptized infants." [11]

With amazing daring she goes on to prophesy that her activity will embrace the entire Church. "I will help priests, missionaries, the whole Church." [12] Further, her mission is to be worldwide: "I will scatter roses on the whole world, upon the just and upon the sinners." [13] What is the explanation of this shower of roses, this rain of graces? It is her unbounded love for Our Blessed Lord and for the souls for whom he shed his Precious Blood and whom she will win to love him. "Heaven to me is to love and to be loved and to return to earth to make Love loved." [14] Finally, she says these astonishing words: "Yes, I know it, all the world will love me." [15]

If the prophecies of St. Thérèse were definite and startling, their fulfilment was equally so. No sooner had she died than a rain of favours fell upon the world. Miracles and graces innumerable spread with a rapidity probably unique in the history of the Church, unparalleled at any rate in recent centuries, until at last there was no part of the Catholic world in which miracles had not happened at her intercession or where favours had not been received by those who invoked her. And along with those favours went the imagery of the rose.

The Holy See tells us that the rain of graces was one of the most weighty factors which led to the rapid canonization of the Saint. In nearly all the more important documents in the process of Beatification and Canonization the Holy See

[8] Ibid., p. 32.
[9] Ibid., p. 77.
[10] Ibid., p. 59.
[11] Ibid., p. 32.
[12] Ibid., p. 62.
[13] Ibid., p. 137.
[14] Ibid., p. 79.
[15] Ibid., p. 100.

makes reference to this rain of graces and, in doing so, invariably uses the imagery of St. Thérèse by referring to it as the "shower of roses".

In the discourse which he delivered on the occasion of the proclamation of the Saint's heroic virtue, Pope Benedict XV says:

Sister Thérèse of the Child Jesus, not long before her death, promised that she would spend her heaven in doing good upon earth. We know that she has fulfilled her promise, because the graces attributed to her intercession have been innumerable.... May the roses promised by Thérèse fall in more abundant measure on that blessed Carmel in which she found satisfaction for all the burning desires of her heart.[16]

The Beatification of St. Thérèse took place on April 29, 1923. In May, Cardinal Vico, Prefect of the Sacred Congregation of Rites, was sent by the Holy Father as Pontifical Legate to preside over the solemnities at Lisieux. In a letter to the Legate, the Holy Father, Pope Pius XI, wrote the following words: "We propose her then to the Children of the Church as a most remarkable example well worthy of imitation. We propose her to them as a heroine of sanctity, and we invoke her as patroness and advocate that she may also continue, as she has begun and as she foretold, to send down a shower of roses from heaven upon mankind." [17]

In the Bull of Canonization, reference is again made to this promise and to its fulfilment: "When dying she had promised to send down an unending shower of roses, that is, a rain of graces; scarcely had she entered heaven when, by innumerable miracles which increased from day to day, she fulfilled her promise." [18]

---

[16] *Story of the Canonization*, pp. 62–63.

[17] Ibid., p. 114.

[18] Ibid., p. 148.

But it is in St. Peter's, on the occasion of the Canonization, that the image of the rose is shown most dramatically to be inseparable from the mission of St. Thérèse. The great basilica was packed to the doors; over two hundred thousand, unable to gain entrance, thronged the piazza outside; the Holy Father, Pope Pius XI, had just ended his homily, in which he said: "That on entering the heavenly country she began her work among souls is clearly manifest when we look at the mystical shower of roses which God permitted and still permits her to let fall upon the earth, as she had so ingenuously promised." [19] Scarcely had he spoken those words when, in full view of the huge assembly, five roses which were decorating a cluster of lights in the apse detached themselves in some unknown way, and floated in wide circles until they rested at the Pontiff's feet. As a background to the scene, there hung the great banner of the Canonization unveiled high above the high altar, and on the banner was depicted boldly the figure of the new Saint, ascending on the clouds to heaven, scattering roses on the earth that she was leaving.

It is typical that God should allow this vital point in St. Thérèse's message to be thus vividly dramatized in St. Peter's, the heart of the Catholic Church, at the moment of the Saint's greatest glory. Thus was it shown to all the world that the words "After my death I will send down a shower of roses" were a prophecy inspired directly by Almighty God.

On the day following the Canonization, the Holy Father, speaking to the pilgrims from Lisieux, said: "Since her intercession is so powerful, what can you not hope to obtain at her hands, thanks to her who promised the roses?" [20] Again the next day, addressing another band of pilgrims, he refers to the same subject: "The little, the great St. Thérèse remains

[19] Ibid., p. 136.
[20] *Autobiography*, p. 276.

beyond the blue sky to shower the roses we are entitled to expect inasmuch as she has promised them."[21] So ended the solemnities in Rome, and thus was fulfilled another of little Thérèse's prophecies, for she was now—in the words of Pope Pius XI—"the child loved throughout the whole world".[22]

Pope Pius XI never hesitated to make use of the symbol of the rose. On September 30, 1925, Cardinal Vico was again Pontifical Legate at the ceremonies of the Canonization at Lisieux. On that occasion the Holy Father gave him a golden rose to place in the hand of the statue of the Saint recumbent on her tomb. On one of the petals were engraved the arms of Pope Pius XI, and the stem bore this inscription: *Auream rosam ab ipso benedictam tibi gratulatus offert Pius XI per manus Eminentis Legati Cardi. Vico S.R.C. Praef. pridie Kal. Oct. MCMXXV.*[23]

From the earliest days of his papacy right up to his death, Pope Pius XI continually spoke of the favours he received from St. Thérèse as "roses"; the best-known instance is, of course, his temporary restoration to health towards the end of his life. Being unable, on account of the pressure of his duties, to be present as he had hoped at Lisieux, for the inauguration of the basilica, the Holy Father sent Cardinal Pacelli, Secretary of State, as his Legate. On the morning of July 11, 1937, on the great square at the entrance to the basilica, in the presence of two hundred and fifty thousand pilgrims, the Legate delivered his discourse, in which he said: "The Supreme Pontiff does not wish to see his ambassador, whom he has sent to you entrusted with his fatherly blessing, return to him with empty hands. 'Bring me back three roses from Lisieux, that is

[21] Ibid., p. 277.

[22] August Pierre Laveille, *St. Thérèse de l'Enfant Jésus* (Clonmore and Reynolds), p. 423.

[23] *Pie XI et son Etoile* (Ed. Carmel of Lisieux), p. 72.

to say, three special graces which we beg of the dear little Saint.' That is what he said to me." [24] The Legate then went on to describe the three roses: the first, a red rose surrounded with thorns, signifying a perfect conformity with the will of God even in the midst of suffering; the second, a yellow rose, signifying the desire of the Holy Father for a complete recovery of his physical health, not in order to avoid suffering, but that he might labour once again for the glory of God and for the good of souls; the third, a white rose, signifying the Holy Father's prayer for holiness of life and fervour for all priests.

At the close of the ceremony the Holy Father gave a broadcast message to the assembled throng and ended it with a reference to his restoration to health, using these words: "The divine King, who loves to dwell with the simple and takes His delight among the lilies, could not but grant this other rose at the intercession of St. Thérèse of the Child Jesus, who has been constantly invoked, as we well know, by the sisters of her family both natural and supernatural." [25]

In view of the fact that the Holy See, so far from discounting or discouraging the imagery of the rose, has been most careful to emphasize and preserve it, we shall not be surprised to find that it still persists wherever St. Thérèse is involved or her Little Way loved and followed. Sometimes, as we have already seen, it is easily explained by natural causes— a bunch of roses, or a single rose, is received by one of St. Thérèse's clients in the most ordinary manner: it comes either during a novena to the Saint, or at a time when the person who receives it has been asking her help over some special trial, or some new venture for God's glory. At other times it is the appearance of a rose petal, or a scent of roses occurring in a way for which there is no natural explanation. In all these cases

[24] *Story of the Canonization*, pp. 89–90.
[25] *Les Annales*, August 1937, p. 228.

it seems to be a sign of the Saint's active interest and approval, for the prayer is usually quickly granted, though not necessarily in the way expected.

What, then, is Almighty God's purpose in all this? First, we may safely take what the Holy See has said:

This young girl was known to few during her lifetime, but immediately after her precious death her fame was spread abroad throughout the Christian world on account of the innumerable wonders wrought by Almighty God at her intercession. Indeed it seemed as if, in accordance with her dying promise, she was sending amongst men her shower of roses. Hence it came to pass that the Church decided to bestow upon her the supreme honour of the Saints without observing the customary and established delays.[26]

God designed that St. Thérèse should not only be raised to the altars of the Church but that she should be so raised in a manner as rapid and as striking as possible. To that end he presented her to his Church as one whose gift of working miracles was unparalleled in its universality and rapidity; and in doing so he showed her to us as scattering roses, which is how the Holy See wishes us to see her today.

By the rain of miracles and graces which he has ordained shall be known as the shower of roses, God has set his seal upon St. Thérèse and her mission. By these miracles, from the very moment of her death, he has been insistently calling the attention of the faithful to the sanctity of St. Thérèse and to her particular type of sanctity, holding it up to the faithful for imitation. He is doing so no less insistently now. The shower of roses is not an end in itself; it is Almighty God pointing the faithful to the Saint and saying: Look well, for this child comes from me to teach you the secret of sanctity.

[26] *Story of the Canonization*, p. 143.

She has been sent to lead us back to the *yet more excellent way*,[27] the way of love. She took as her motto those words of St. John of the Cross, "Love is repaid by Love alone", and she explained what this meant to her:

> Well do I know it, my God! And therefore I have sought and found a way to ease my heart by giving Thee love for love . . . but how shall I show my love, since love proves itself by deeds? I, the little child, will strew flowers perfuming the Divine Throne with their fragrance. Thus will my short life be spent in Thy sight, O my Beloved!
>
> To strew flowers is the only means I have of proving my love for Thee; that is to say, I will let no little sacrifice escape me, not a look, not a word, I will make use of the smallest actions and I will do them all for love.
>
> For love's sake I suffer and for love's sake I will rejoice; thus will I strew my flowers.
>
> Not one that I see, but singing all the while, I will scatter its petals before Thee. Should my roses be scattered from amid thorns, I will sing notwithstanding, and the longer and sharper the thorns, the sweeter will grow my song.[28]

The profound truth of this passage leaves us silent. It is a passage for meditation rather than for exposition. Yet we must attempt some comment, for we are here at the central secret of the Little Way: it is the way of little sacrifices. It cannot be emphasised too strongly that the whole of her teaching is based on trust and self-surrender—a self-surrender in which no sacrifice is ever to be considered too small or too great. The most trifling actions done out of love, and done cheerfully, are of great value in the eyes of God.

---

[27] I Cor 12:31.
[28] *Autobiography*, p. 206.

Jeter des fleurs! . . . c'est t'offrir en prémices
Les plus légers soupirs, les plus grandes douleurs.
Mes peines, mon bonheur, mes petits sacrifices,
    Voilà mes fleurs. [29]

Thérèse goes yet further: *she herself* will become like a flower given in sacrifice; she will become the rose that is laid at his feet, that is to say, her life will become one act of perfect love for Our Lord. This analogy is developed in her poem "La Rose effeuillée".[30] In it she describes how she lays a rose before the Infant Jesus so that, supported by his Mother's arms in his first attempt to walk, he may rest his feet upon it.

Jesus, to aid thy feeble powers,
    I see thy Mother's arms outspread,
As thou on this sad earth of ours
    Dost set thy first, thy faltering tread;
See, in thy path I cast away
    A rose in all its beauty dressed,
That on its petals' disarray
    Thy feet, so light, may softly rest.

This fallen rose, she says, is the image of a heart consumed by love. There are many beautiful flowers on the altar, but she does not want to be one of them: she wants to be a rose whose petals are scattered at the feet of Jesus, all its beauty lost and forgotten.

Dear Infant Christ, this fallen rose
    An image of that heart should be

---

[29] "Each passing sigh, each bitter sorrow,/ My joys, my suffering,/ Each little sacrifice Thou askest/ These are the flowers I bring."—"Jeter des fleurs", *Poems*. Translated by Msgr. R. A. Knox.

[30] The French text will be found in full at the end of this chapter

Which makes, as every instant flows,
    Its whole burnt-sacrifice to thee.
Upon thy altars, Lord, there gleams
    Full many a flower whose grand display
Charms thee; but I have other dreams. . . .
    Bloomless, to cast myself away.

Dear Lord, the flowers that blossom yet
    Thy feast-day with their perfume fill;
The rose that's fallen, men forget,
    The winds may scatter where they will;
The rose that's fallen questions not,
    Content, as for thy sake, to die,
Abandonment its welcome lot
    Dear infant Christ, that rose be I!

She will lie at his feet, content to die for him, confident
that the beauty of the petals, as they lie scattered here and there
by the will of God, will far surpass any beauty they once had
in mortal eyes.

Yet those same petals, trampled down . . .
    I read the message in my heart . . .
In patterns here and there are blown
    That seem too beautiful for art:
Living to mortal eyes no more,
    Rose of a bloom for ever past,
See to thy love a life made o'er,
    A future on thy mercy cast!

For love of Loveliness supreme,
    Dying, to cast myself away
Were bright fulfilment of my dream;
    I'd prove my love no easier way:

> *Live, here below, forgotten still,*
>   *A rose before thy path outspread*
> *At Nazareth, or on Calvary's hill*
>   *Relieve thy last, thy labouring tread.*[31]

And so, with a life of beauty and sacrifice known only to Jesus, she will prove her love by an act of total abandonment and thus slake his thirst for souls, minister to his wounds, and *fill up those things that are wanting of the sufferings of Christ.* Abandonment to the providence of God in all the details of life, this is at once the sternest and the most consoling lesson of the spiritual life; for those who follow the way of Spiritual Childhood there will be joy, but a joy that is born of suffering. And what is this but an echo of Our Lord's own words? *Take up my yoke upon you and learn of me, for my yoke is sweet and my burden light.*

LA ROSE EFFEUILLÉE

> *Jésus, quand je te vois, soutenu par ta Mère,*
>   *Quitter ses bras,*
> *Essayer en tremblant sur notre triste terre*
>   *Tes premiers pas;*
> *Devant toi je voudrais effeuiller une rose*
>   *En sa fraîcheur,*
> *Pour que ton petit pied bien doucement repose*
>   *Sur une fleur.*
>
> *Cette rose effeuillée est la fidèle image,*
>   *Divin Enfant,*
> *Du cœur qui veut pour toi s'immoler sans partage,*
>   *A chaque instant.*

---

[31] "La Rose effeuillée", *Poems*, p. 52. Translated by Msgr. R. A. Knox.

Seigneur, sur tes autels plus d'une fraîche rose
Aime à briller;
Elle se donne à toi, mais je rêve autre chose:
C'est m'effeuiller...

La rose en son éclat peut embellir ta fête,
Aimable Enfant!
Mais la rose effeuillée, on l'oublie, on la jette
Au gré du vent
La rose, en s'effeuillant, sans recherche se donne
Pour n'être plus.
Comme elle, avec bonheur, à toi je m'abandonne,
Petit Jésus!

L'on marche sans regret sur des feuilles de rose,
Et ces débris
Sont un simple ornement que sans art on dispose,
Je l'ai compris...
Jésus, pour ton amour j'ai prodigué ma vie,
Mon avenir;
Aux regards des mortels, rose à jamais flétrie,
Je dois mourir!

Pour toi je dois mourir, Jésus, beauté suprême,
Oh! quel bonheur!
Je veux en m'effeuillant te prouver que je t'aime
De tout mon cœur.
Sous tes pas enfantins, je veux avec mystère
Vivre ici-bas;
Et je voudrais encor adoucir au Calvaire
Tes derniers pas...

APPENDIX

HOW ST. THÉRÈSE FOUND
A PRIEST-BROTHER

THE CONVERSION STORY OF FATHER VERNON JOHNSON

by Sister Marie Immanuel, S.C.

"She has received a mission to teach priests a greater love of Jesus Christ."—Pope Benedict XV

St. Thérèse of Lisieux herself frequently spoke of her intense desire to offer her life that priests might be holy, praying not only for her two adopted missionary "brothers", but for all priests. That her concern for priestly souls continues, though Thérèse has long since left Carmel for heaven, is shown in the unusual story of Father Vernon Johnson, who, when the Little Flower first entered his life, was a priest in the Anglican Church and a friar in an Anglo-Catholic religious order.

To appreciate what wonders Thérèse worked for Friar Vernon in bringing him to Rome, one must understand how firmly he was entrenched in Anglo-Catholicism. His sister's account of his life before he encountered Thérèse makes it clear how impossible it would have seemed to Father Vernon himself or to those who knew him best that he would ever be touched by "Roman fever".

He had hardly ever been inside a Catholic church; he knew no Catholic priests, and he experienced no uneasiness about his attraction to things Roman, considering it simply a

Reprinted with permission of *Immaculata* magazine and the Conventual Franciscan Friars of Marytown.

treasured inheritance from the Oxford Movement. But Miss Johnson's account also details the popular young friar's love for Christ and for his poorest ones, as well as his gifts as preacher and spiritual director.

Vernon Johnson was born into a well-to-do English family in 1886. He entered an Episcopalian seminary from college to study for the priesthood. Ordained in 1910, his first assignment was curate in the desolate slums of Brighton, a coastal town in England. Three arduous years there, however, left him unsatisfied; things were still "too easy", and he longed for the stricter discipline of a religious order. Consequently, in the spring of 1914 he entered the Anglo-Catholic Society of Divine Compassion, and, after a brief formation period, Father Vernon, wearing a Franciscan habit, set off on his first assignment as a religious. It was an assignment that gives some measure of his priestly character even then: with another friar and two nurses he was to open and direct a home for English lepers. Two years later, Saint Giles was a well-established hospice where England's few lepers were welcomed with love to spend their remaining days in dignity and peace.

From Saint Giles, Father Vernon was sent to London's East End, "a dark and frightening place," wrote Miss Johnson, "where poverty and misery dwelt and men fought for mere existence". Father Vernon had barely settled there when the Spanish flu, epidemic throughout Europe, was carried to England and raged unconfined through the slums. The Brothers from the East End House of Divine Compassion, acting as undertakers for the poor, often buried fifty people a day before returning to the poor dwellings to pray with the dying and comfort the bereaved.

To add to the distress of those months, devastating raids by enemy aircraft often brought incalculable destruction to the

thickly-populated neighborhood, where the flimsy houses
offered little protection from fire or bombs. Since in the East
End there were no established places of refuge from air attacks,
Father Vernon and the other Brothers went from house to
house to be with their people during those awful hours. After
the final air raid, in May 1918, the Brothers returned to their
little House of Compassion to find that it had been completely
demolished; only the crucifix was left, still hanging on a shat-
tered door.

After the war, Father Vernon served in different houses of
his society. becoming much sought after both as a preacher
and as a spiritual director. Canon Gordon Albion, in a biog-
raphical sketch, noted that "his good looks were enhanced by
his Franciscan habit and still more by his innate sense of style
and flair in the pulpit, bringing him crowds of young socialites
and debutantes to hear him preach." Thérèse must have rec-
ognized that it was high time she intervened. And so it happened that, when Father Vernon went to a convent to make
a retreat, late in 1924, the first rose was sent tumbling down
to him: the Anglican sister in charge of the house offered him
The Story of a Soul for his spiritual reading.

Father Vernon demurred. "No, thanks", he said, handing
it back. "It's French—and it's Roman Catholic." "Don't be
prejudiced", the sister admonished. "Take it and read it: you'll
like it."

Humbly, Father Vernon took the autobiography to his
room. The first two chapters did not reassure him: in fact, he
found them distressingly cloying, just as he had expected. His
first impression, he told a friend later, was, "What an appalling
pious little prig!" But he read on, and then— then Thérèse
began to emerge, and Father Vernon read until early morning, read until he had turned the last page. The simple story
moved him as no other book ever had. Five years later, try-

ing to explain to stunned friends why he was submitting to
Rome, he wrote of that first encounter with Thérèse:

> Here was someone who had loved Our Lord to a degree
> beyond anything I had ever seen before: a love as strong as
> that of the martyrs of old and yet with the delicacy and ten-
> derness of a little child, so delicate and tender that one
> almost fails to realize the furnace in which that love was
> wondrously refined. Above all else, it was the Saint's gospel
> of suffering as being the most blessed gift, by which alone
> we could be really united to our Blessed Lord in unfettered
> love, and her interpretation of pain and suffering as some-
> thing which can be offered in union with our Blessed Lord's
> cross for the sake of the Church and for the salvation of
> souls—it was all this which, coming into my life when
> things were exceedingly difficult, lit up and made real to
> me certain spiritual truths towards which I was dimly grop-
> ing; truths which I had been discouraged from holding as
> being morbid and so forth, and which I now found were
> the very foundations of the saintly life.... For over six
> months the study of this book pulled me through one of
> the most difficult passages of my life.

"I find here my own thoughts, word for word my own spiritual experiences", he confided to his beloved sister while discussing the book with her. "From that moment," she
remembered, "he had no peace. Five crucifying years were to
pass before he could take the irrevocable step that knowing
Thérèse had made mandatory for him. He went to Lisieux
with other pilgrims. "My first impression", he wrote, "was one
of great repulsion; it was all so foreign, sentimental and
artificial." But the sense of strangeness, the disappointment,
left him in the Carmelites' Hall of Relics. There, he was
deeply moved to see so many things Thérèse had used during her brief religious life.

His visit to Les Buissonnets, Thérèse's childhood home, was also a touching experience. He did not need a guide as he moved from room to room; the autobiography had made everything familiar. Like other tourists, he looked reverently at the mementos, all carefully shielded behind glass partitions—her copybook, her rosary, her own small desk, her skipping rope, and top. The contrast between the toys and the scourge he had seen at the convent seemed to Father Vernon to epitomize the story of Thérèse's life, "a perfect parable of the power of Divine Grace". He was charmed by the pretty walled garden, too, recalling how Thérèse as a little girl had spent happy hours there, playing or "thinking". He did not dream that the next day would find him a prisoner there, yet that is what happened. For his little Saint, in her own characteristic way, had set out to secure a special favor for her client, now that he was actually in Lisieux: a private meeting with the prioress, Mother Agnes of Jesus, Thérèse's beloved "little Mother".

Consequently, when Father Vernon returned to the garden late that afternoon to pray, the sister-guardian, not realizing that there were still guests on the premises, locked the garden gate and all the doors, pocketed the keys, and went off. To the staid Father Vernon's chagrin, he and a young Belgian priest who had joined him in the garden and with whom he had been lost in conversation, had to seek a ladder, scale the wall, and then, by making a most unseemly racket, attract the attention of neighbors who could assist them down from their high perches.

Because of the misadventure, Father Vernon was late for dinner at the hotel. Because he was late, he was seated with a newcomer. Because the newcomer insisted that they visit the cemetery where Thérèse's mother is buried, Father Vernon grudgingly accompanied him. Because he was in the cemetery just at that time, he encountered a woman tending a grave who introduced herself as a classmate of the Saint. Because the woman took an interest in the Protestant clergyman from England, she offered to try to arrange for him to speak with Mother Agnes. And because the Little Flower was undoubtedly pushing the whole affair, Mother Agnes agreed to meet with him, although the nuns had not been granting interviews that week due to canonization business!

The next morning found Father Vernon kneeling at the white-curtained grille in the little parlor where Thérèse as a child had knelt in floods of tears, talking to this same loved sister. Father Vernon opened his heart to her. "You must react", she told him. But he dismissed the advice without a scruple, sure that the holy Roman Catholic nun did not realize that he, as an Anglo-Catholic, already enjoyed and treasured everything that Rome could offer him: the Mass, the sacraments, Our Lady, even religious life, which he had been living for years in various houses of Divine Compassion as a Franciscan friar. Nevertheless, that brief visit was the spiritual highlight of his entire pilgrimage, and he was sure he owed it to Thérèse.

"I was conscious", he wrote years later, "that my visit was being guided in a mysterious way. At first, it seemed coincidence...but as time went on, I knew it was more than mere coincidence which led me, a stranger and all unknown, to kneel in the Carmel parlor and receive the blessing of Mother Agnes, the Saint's own sister; I must believe it was the prayers of the little Saint herself."

Though Father Vernon was back in London in less than a week he realized that he had been through a spiritual experience unlike anything he had ever known before. What he had encountered firsthand, he knew, was a love of God such as he had never met before. "The deity of Christ", he said, "was flashed before my soul at Lisieux with blinding splendor. My soul drank deep there at the pure stream of the undiluted truth of the Godhead of my Lord. . . . I had been where the unseen was very, very near, and where the veil was very, very thin."

The Catholic Church as such, however, did not attract him even then. His experience gave him no desire to become a Catholic and no thought that he would ever be one. He went home resolving, instead, to try to make devotion to Christ in the Blessed Sacrament, as he had seen it at Lisieux and knew it in Thérèse's life, "the very life and breath of the Church of England".

And with that resolution, he settled down again to work for souls as an Anglican religious.

"I Shall Be a Catholic"

A year later Father Johnson returned to Lisieux. His second visit made him aware that he could no longer evade the challenges he met there. *Was* the Church that had produced a Saint Thérèse of the Child Jesus, he asked himself a thousand times over, the *true* Church? Here, apparently, was real sanctity: How was that possible in the context of the modern world? Besides, such sanctity must have been rooted in the absolutism of faith, which in turn would depend on the living authority of the Church. Could he find that authority in the Church of England? As he said good-bye after this second visit, he told the nuns soberly, "When I come back, I shall be a Catholic." But he admitted later that he simply couldn't contemplate ever taking such a step.

After Father Johnson's death, his sister explained just what "going over to Rome" had cost him. "It meant a clean break", she wrote. "Church, career, friends, all had to be sacrificed.

Above all, the thought of his flock troubled him. the thousands of souls who followed him.... He had to leave them all, and none of them would understand the step he was taking. The many people who afterwards condemned him for his selfishness had no idea of the *via dolorosa* of those years."

For a sensitive nature like Father Vernon's, the pain resulting from the mere thought of hurting those who loved him was almost unbearable. He confided to the Carmelites at Lisieux that he often woke at night crying to God, "You cannot ask this of me: I cannot do it!" But an even more sacred obligation was holding him back: the role that he perhaps should play in the rapidly increasing evidence of Catholic life in the Church of England, for example, in the extraordinary increase in the number of English contemplatives.

A Seminarian Again at Age Forty-three

Characteristically, while Father Vernon prayed and deliberated and suffered, Thérèse continued her delicate little attentions. (She definitely would *not* take no for an answer!) Finally, five years after he had first opened her autobiography, and three years after his second trip to Lisieux had overwhelmed him with doubts, Vernon Johnson was received into the Catholic Church. Then, leaving everything he had known and loved, he went to Rome to begin at forty-three his preparation for the Catholic priesthood.

During his long course of studies at the Beda, Saint Thérèse's seminarian delved deeper into the mysteries of her Little Way, struggling to incorporate it into every area of his life, to build his prayer on it to share it with others. From the start, he had seen in it what many of Thérèse's admirers never grasp: that Thérèse's Way is the way of the Cross, utilizing suffering for holiness.

Now, he discovered that it was primarily a gospel message, too, based on Our Lord's own words, "Unless you become as little children, you shall not enter the kingdom of heaven." Important also was the papal approval: the new convert was doggedly loyal to the Holy See. And it was a Pauline way; he rejoiced in that Thérèse often quoted Saint Paul, and Vernon quoted both of them, becoming more and more aware of just what Thérèse had to say to him, to priests, and to all the faithful.

In June 1933, at the age of forty-nine, Vernon Johnson went home to England to be ordained a Catholic priest, and within a fortnight he was in Lisieux, to say Mass for the nuns who had done so much to pray him toward his goal. Thérèse intervened again, this time with a favor he had never dreamed of: the bishop of Lisieux, whom he met unexpectedly, gave him permission to visit inside the cloister, a privilege so rare as to be almost unheard of. As the cloister door was unbolted for him, he dropped to his knees to kiss the sill—Thérèse had entered through that doorway the day she came to Carmel. That blessed afternoon he was permitted to pray to his heart's content in her tiny cell, in the chapter room where she had made her vows, and in the choir where she had spent so many hours every day. Thérèse's culminating ordination gift came the next morning: he was invited to offer his Mass in the bare little infirmary room where she had suffered and died, using the chalice Thérèse had so often handled when she was sacristan, the one she holds in the photograph, so often seen, of her in the sacristy. "In that hour", wrote his sister, he "regained his peace."

What Father Johnson did for and with St. Thérèse in his three happy decades in the Catholic priesthood makes another story, for he dedicated his life to spreading her Little Way, especially carrying on her apostolate to priests, organizing the

Association of the Priests of St. Thérèse, editing *Sicut Parvuli*, a quarterly review for the associates, and spending himself in giving retreats and days of recollection steeped in the Thérèsian theology so geared to priestly needs.

The Rosary, His Source of Comfort

Another story might center on his lifelong love of Our Lady, which burgeoned under Thérèse's tutelage until, in the weakness of old age, he had his rosary always in his hands, finding in it a constant source of comfort and his final quiet effort to walk Thérèse's Little Way to God. The sister-nurse who was with him on night duty in his illness recalled that, toward the end, visitors tired him quickly, but he never tired of having someone pray the Rosary with him and would always thank the visitor for his kindness.

Mindful to the last of St. Thérèse's desire to bring priests closer to Christ, he said wistfully to his nurse just before he died, "Sister, I don't feel that I've done as much as I should have done for priests." She reassured him, and he smiled and said, "Thank you, Sister! Now I am very happy." Those were his last words. He died in 1969 at the age of eighty. Thérèse's protégé had used well the roses she had showered down on him for so many years!